Praise for *The 3 Power Values*

"I have seen David Gebler put these powerful ideas into action, and they work."

—**Shira Goodman**, executive vice president,
human resources, Staples, Inc.

"Illuminating, compelling, and actionable. A true contribution for leaders navigating the complex intersection of company performance, values, compliance, people, and organizational behavior."

—**Kim Rucker**, senior vice president and general counsel,
Avon Products, Inc.

"A must-read. I have worked with David Gebler for over seven years, and with *The 3 Power Values* he is once again at the forefront of driving positive cultural change in organizations."

—**Vincent Brockman**, executive vice president,
general counsel, and chief ethics and compliance officer,
Scotts Miracle-Gro Company

"David Gebler's book draws as much on his decades of hands-on experience working with companies on their ethical challenges as it does on his keen insight into the three values—commitment, integrity, and transparency—that drive any company's performance. It's essential reading for all managers striving to understand their corporate culture and create a high-performing organization."

—**Jeffrey Seglin**, author, *The Right Thing: Conscience, Profit, and Personal Responsibility in Today's Business*

"*The 3 Power Values* is a must-read for every manager. Creating a culture of trust and commitment is crucial for any institution to survive long term. Yet sustaining cooperation internally and maintaining a reputation for trustworthiness is complex. *The 3 Power Values* is a clear and unique guide to creating and maintaining such a culture. It is simple without being simplistic, and convincing without being rigid and inflexible."

—**Tamar Frankel**, professor of law, Boston University School of Law; author, *Trust and Honesty: America's Business Culture at a Crossroad*

"A breakthrough, commonsense primer for establishing effective corporate cultures to assist employees in avoiding costly and destructive ethical and legal lapses. A compelling read for corporate leaders in today's heavily regulated and overly litigious environment."

—**Harvey L. Pitt**, CEO of global strategic business consultancy, Kalorama Partners; 26th Chairman of the U.S. Securities and Exchange Commission

THE 3 POWER VALUES

How Commitment, Integrity, and Transparency Clear the Roadblocks to Performance

DAVID GEBLER

JOSSEY-BASS
A Wiley Imprint
www.josseybass.com

Published by Jossey-Bass
A Wiley Imprint
One Montgomery Street, Suite 1200
San Francisco, CA 94104-4594
www.josseybass.com

Jossey-Bass books and products are available through most bookstores. To contact Jossey-Bass directly call our Customer Care Department within the U.S. at 800-956-7739, outside the U.S. at 317-572-3986, or fax 317-572-4002.

Wiley publishes in a variety of print and electronic formats and by print-on-demand. Some material included with standard print versions of this book may not be included in e-books or in print-on-demand. If this book refers to media such as a CD or DVD that is not included in the version you purchased, you may download this material at http://booksupport.wiley.com. For more information about Wiley products, visit www.wiley.com.

Library of Congress Cataloging-in-Publication Data

Gebler, David.
    The 3 power values : how commitment, integrity, and transparency clear the roadblocks to performance / by David Gebler.—1st ed.
        p. cm.
    Includes bibliographical references and index.
    ISBN 978-1-118-10132-2 (hardback); ISBN 978-1-118-22384-0 (ebk);
ISBN 978-1-118-23712-0 (ebk); ISBN 978-1-118-26213-9 (ebk)
    1. Commitment (Psychology) 2. Integrity. 3. Corporate
culture. 4. Organization. I. Title. II. Title: Three power values.
    BF619.G43 2012
    650.1—dc23

                                                2011050767

Printed in the United States of America

FIRST EDITION

HB Printing   10 9 8 7 6 5 4 3 2 1

For Claire

CONTENTS

Preface   *ix*

PART 1: ALIGNMENT IS THE KEY   1

1   Culture Drives Performance   3
2   Behavior Roadblocks   32
3   Values Drive Culture   59

PART 2: THE POWER VALUES   89

4   Integrity Aligns Goals and Standards   91
5   Commitment Aligns Principles and Goals   117
6   Transparency Aligns Principles and Standards   145
7   Your Plan for High Performance   170

Notes   *199*
Suggested Readings   *207*
Acknowledgments   *209*
About the Author   *211*
Index   *213*

PREFACE

It might seem unusual, but the origins of this book stem from a comic strip. In the early 1990s, I was cofounder of a small consulting firm that was among the first licensees for the new *Dilbert* comic strip. Having secured the rights to use Scott Adams's characters for internal communications and training, we worked with companies that were trying to be open and self-effacing about their challenges. I began to see a fascinating gap: everybody knew there were issues facing their company, but no one seemed to be willing to talk about them. In fact, *Dilbert* strips became the language by which employees could communicate their feelings. People wouldn't say anything to their manager, but they would post a comic strip on their door or cubicle wall.

Several of the early classic strips mocked Dilbert's company's core values. I thought a lot about why that was so funny. The values, such as integrity and trust, were good and important concepts. So what made them such perfect targets for satiric irony? The employees wanted these values. The organization said it wanted these values. What was happening in the middle to make such a joke—and such a mess—of it?

I carried this puzzlement with me as I began to help organizations develop ethics and compliance programs. Companies that wanted to reduce and prevent misconduct kept falling back on check-the-box compliance training that basically told employees: "These are the standards of behavior that are expected of you." It soon became clear that employees rarely needed to be told that they should do the right thing or even to be told what the rules were. They knew all that. What they needed was help in removing the frustrations and pressures that could cause a good person to do a bad thing. As I dug more deeply, it also became clear to me that the root cause of ethics issues was also the root cause that kept an organization's performance weaker than it needed to be or made it hard to motivate employees who really wanted to be engaged and committed to the company. At the heart of performance is the environment in which employees work: the culture.

Culture was clearly having an impact on performance, and yet leaders were not seeing it. I felt like the little boy in the fable who was the only one willing to shout that the emperor was not wearing any clothes. Why is it so hard to say what needs to be said? I saw that most organizations did not have a systematic way to look at their culture so that they could make the changes needed to improve performance.

One of the challenges for leaders who want to influence their culture is that culture cuts across many disciplines. The task of understanding culture requires the best thinking in leadership, ethics, organizational development, behavioral science, and psychology. Extensive new research over the past twenty-five years or so has helped uncover the factors that influence behavior. Classic social psychology has always had insights into how to create an effective and high-performing culture. There is plenty of information on this topic but not many strategies for organizing the data so a leader can develop a coherent plan. If you are like most other leaders, you know that you should look at culture and that improving the work environment will improve performance and reduce the risks that bad things will happen. But you don't know where to start. And one reason is that you do not have a workable model of culture that will help you change how people go about their work.

The 3 Power Values presents a new way of looking at culture that is geared to helping managers and leaders make the link to performance. I present a model of how various elements of culture can either work together to create a high-performing organization or work at cross-purposes, creating dysfunction that can lead to poor performance or even misconduct.

From my twenty years of experience working with large and small organizations across the globe, I have learned that employees already embody the values needed to create a high-performing culture. Leaders do not need to invent a culture. They just need to get out of the way of their people creating one naturally. I found that every organization has key levers that managers can use to influence the behaviors that drive culture. Behaviors associated with three values—commitment, integrity, and transparency—remove the behavior-based roadblocks that keep people from being able to live their values at work. That's when corporate core values stop being a joke.

Culture change needs to be supported from the top of the organization, but it needs to be implemented in the field. This book is for every manager or leader who feels the need to create a more effective team, unit, division, or organization. I offer you practical advice and guidance, gleaned from my work with global organizations, on how to make changes in your organization's culture that will improve its operational and ethical performance.

Throughout the book, I refer to people, employees, managers, and leaders. When I speak about the "people" in an organization or about "employees" generally, I am referring to everyone who works in an organization, from hourly employees through senior leadership. I use "line employees" if I am referring to employees who do not manage others. When I speak of "leaders," I intend to include anyone who manages others, from a frontline supervisor to the CEO. If I am intending to refer to senior executives, the context will make that clear. I shy away from distinguishing "managers" from "leaders," because every manager is a leader and each has his or her own set of responsibilities and role to play in managing the culture.

Removing the roadblocks to performance is a journey. The successful companies are the ones that focus less attention on what the final destination will look like—too many things can change along the way—and more on how they are going to get there with their mission, their skills, their profits, and their principles intact.

Let's get started.

Sharon, Massachusetts   David Gebler
February 2012

THE 3 POWER VALUES

PART 1

Alignment Is the Key

Culture Drives Performance

The quality engineer couldn't believe what he was hearing. In 2005, when a sample from a batch of more than a million bottles of St. Joseph aspirin wouldn't dissolve properly, the engineer did what Johnson & Johnson quality professionals had been doing for generations: he blocked that batch from shipping. Now he was being chewed out by his boss. "Do you like working here?" the manager asked. "Then make sure this shipment passes. There's no reason it should fail."[1]

The engineer thought, *How could this be happening?* Back in the 1980s, quality professionals were the white knights of the company. Entrusted with its reputation and expected to enforce its highest production standards, they were empowered to stop any shipment. But now the company was facing tremendous pressure to cut costs, and harried operations managers were reluctant to throw away millions of bottles of product, so they came down hard on the quality engineers. And sure enough, many of the quality engineers bowed to the pressure. Once honored for their integrity, they now found themselves saying one thing and doing another.

Johnson & Johnson (J&J) had been one of America's most admired companies for over one hundred years. Products such as Band-Aid,

Johnson's Baby Shampoo, and Tylenol were trusted brands. J&J had been praised countless times as one of the best examples of a values-driven organization, relying on the core principles and beliefs embodied in its fabled Credo to guide leaders through tough decisions.[2]

Yet quality standards have been declining since 2000. From 2009 through 2011, J&J's famed consumer products division, McNeil Consumer Healthcare, announced more than a dozen recalls. One was brought on by the presence of metal shavings in children's medicine; another involved 136 million bottles of children's Tylenol, the biggest children's drug recall of all time. In 2009, J&J was even caught attempting what some have termed a "phantom recall." According to the U.S. Food and Drug Administration, J&J hired contractors to buy up defective bottles of Motrin from store shelves rather than publicly announce a recall. This kind of deceptive behavior went beyond mere product quality issues. It signaled that a vast gulf had opened between the company's values and the day-to-day decisions that its employees and managers make. That gulf has proven to be an enormous detriment to the company's reputation, with executives even being publicly scolded in Congress for being "deceptive, dishonest, and [risking] the health of many of our children."[3] As of January 2011, its share in the $4.2 billion cough-and-cold market had fallen from 17 percent to 5 percent.

How could one of the most admired companies of all time squander so many years of accumulated goodwill? Some blame a clash of cultures after global pharmaceutical giant Pfizer's consumer products division was merged into McNeil in 2006; the new organization no longer permitted local leaders to oversee manufacturing and quality. Others point to cost cutting in response to market changes.

Could it be that obvious? Many companies face similar challenges. Leaders are always trying to lower costs and execute strategies more effectively. They are always asking more from their people, who often find themselves working under tremendous pressure. Why do some companies create a toxic internal structure while other companies, under the same circumstances, manage the pressures with a dynamic workforce that stays fully committed to the organization's mission and values?

We may never know exactly what happened at J&J, but we can be fairly certain that it was not an evil cabal of managers lurking in the New Jersey headquarters. There is no evidence of managers who were hell-bent on turning out defective products for personal financial gain. Instead, these were hundreds of managers simply trying to cope with the pressures of doing more with less. And that's what should be so frightening about this story: if you cannot pinpoint the reasons that a company like J&J fails, you cannot set up an adequate strategy to manage performance and ethical risks at your own company.

As you will see, J&J seemed to lose its ability to have a positive influence on how employees went about doing their work and making difficult decisions; that is, it had lost its grip on its own culture. In particular, J&J was not mindful of how three critical values—integrity, commitment, and transparency—need to work together to influence employee behavior in the right direction. J&J managers might not have even known they needed to track these values, but as you will learn in this book, allowing even one of them to fail undermines the other two, allowing the temporizing and self-deceptive aspects of human nature to lead a company down the wrong path. J&J certainly went down that path, losing sight of the kinds of decisions it needed to make to maintain its competitive position in the market.

I will show you that these three values help take culture out of the realm of the soft and nonstrategic and into your familiar world of action plans.

PLACING BLAME VERSUS REMOVING ROADBLOCKS

Leaders are often baffled when a company or a key division underperforms or screws up. I believe the reason is that they often look at the problem from the wrong direction. They typically decide that some particular person, policy, or process was faulty and needs to be reengineered, revised, retrained, or replaced. J&J's solutions to McNeil's string of problems were fairly typical. J&J claims to have addressed its quality problems by replacing McNeil leaders, installing new equipment, and reorganizing the quality department. As I will show in this book, such steps, although they appear to be decisive leadership, are probably addressing the symptoms rather than getting to the heart of the problem. The road to high performance begins with understanding how your company's culture affects your people's behavior and performance.

A company I'll call Lothrop Financial, a major player in the heavily regulated insurance industry, took this approach.[4] A high-potential young manager had been giving her clients the answers to the exam for a federal compliance training program. This was blatantly illegal and would have gotten the company into very serious trouble. The manager was fired, but Lothrop's leadership knew they hadn't solved the problem yet. Many others had known what this manager was doing and had failed to speak up. And yet it is unlikely that those who had kept quiet were notably incompetent or dishonest. What puzzled Lothrop's top executives was that such a violation could occur in the midst of so many people who knew perfectly well what was right and wrong. Lothrop understood that it had a cultural problem on its hands. They didn't know what to do about it, but they knew retraining wasn't enough.

In my work helping organizations identify where their values are either encouraging or hampering performance, I have found that most employees have a strong sense of the values and behaviors that will make for organizational success, for example, fairness and open communication. Employees from top to bottom want to feel committed and connected to the organization and to help it succeed, and most of them are willing to go way beyond their job descriptions to help their company.

What employees and managers often do not know, however, is how to act on those positive values and feelings. Many times they hold back. They think that no one really cares how hard they try. They don't feel empowered to raise issues, ask questions, or bring matters up to higher levels of leadership. They may feel that the collective benefits of raising an issue or asking a question do not outweigh the individual risks of retribution or humiliation. These fears and frustrations are the roadblocks that prevent good people from doing the things that keep companies honest and high performing for the long haul. Such roadblocks can keep a production manager at J&J from taking a safety risk seriously enough or keep a J&J quality engineer from bringing it up in the first place. Such roadblocks kept Lothrop employees quiet while one of their fellows was putting the company at serious risk.

As I will show you, employees who can live their values at work feel engaged and committed. They care how their company does and feel safe raising issues and questioning decisions that run counter to the organization's core principles and beliefs. Their companies are more likely to weather the kind of storms that did so much harm to J&J. There will always be new problems and temptations, so organizations need to foster the qualities that enable employees to resolve whatever comes up, always keeping the organization's values intact.

Your challenge as a leader is not to cajole your employees to do more or to instruct them on how they ought to behave. It is to remove the roadblocks for employees who already want to give the organization their best. In *The 3 Power Values*, I show you how.

CULTURE MATTERS

Every company with employees has a corporate culture. It may be actively cultivated or not even thought about, but it's there, creating and sustaining the social norms that influence behavior. Academics strive for an accurate definition, but most business leaders feel no need to define, measure, or manage culture.[5] I define *culture* as "how we do things around here" in order to focus on the relationship between behavior and the work environment. Company culture can influence behavior positively—as it does for Southwest Airlines, Nordstrom, and Starbucks, which state clear expectations of employee behavior and are generally regarded as achieving exceptional employee performance—or it can set the bar so low that dysfunction or outright misconduct can be the social norm, as you will see happened at WorldCom in Chapter Two.

Many leaders see company culture as no more strategic than an employee picnic, never examining its role in meeting their business objectives. Is something in your company's culture causing—or at least nudging—otherwise good employees to withhold their best efforts or ignore stated rules and policies? Were there changes in J&J's culture— not merely in its business circumstances—that permitted or even encouraged some quality managers and engineers to dance around the Credo? Was there something in Lothrop's culture that allowed or even encouraged an otherwise promising manager who knew the rules to ignore them and cheat on compliance training—and that allowed or even encouraged others to keep quiet about it?

To ignore the influence your organization's culture has on your people's behavior is to ignore the powerful link between how well a company performs and how well its culture aligns with employees' values and its own stated goals. When a company's cultural values do not line up with the values of its employees, the company suffers poor performance, which can take many forms, ranging from the apathy of the staff to the degradation of the company's products and services. When employees feel valued and supported—because the company's cultural values are in line with their own—they enjoy their work and willingly give their best, all to the company's benefit.

Investing in the top twenty publicly traded companies in *Fortune*'s annual "100 Best Companies to Work For" list over the past ten years would have realized an average annualized return of 16.74 percent, compared to 2.83 percent for the S&P 500.[6] A study of 163 organizations, carried out by Hewitt Associates and the Barrett Values Centre as part of the 2008 Best Employer study in Australia/New Zealand, showed that cultural alignment significantly influences employee engagement, which in turn significantly influences organizational and financial performance.[7] Company culture matters. A healthy company culture delivers.

Business leaders do not take a Hippocratic oath to do no harm, but their boards, investors, employees, and customers—not to mention regulators—expect them to keep the company out of legal trouble and its employees and customers out of danger. An aligned company culture has a significant impact on reducing those risks. The Ethics Resource Center (ERC), a nonprofit, nonpartisan organization that studies ethical standards and practices in public and private institutions, found in its 2007 report that only 24 percent of employees in companies with strong ethical cultures observe misconduct, well below the national average and far below the 98 percent who observe misconduct in companies with weak ethical cultures. Only 3 percent of the employees working in companies with strong ethical cultures who reported misconduct experienced retaliation as a result, compared to the 39 percent who experienced retaliation in weak ethical cultures. The ERC concluded that culture has a greater impact than a formal ethics and compliance program on outcomes such as observed misconduct, reporting of misconduct, and perceived ability to handle misconduct if faced with such a situation.[8] Recall Lothrop, which did have a legally defendable compliance program, yet had a big problem with reporting of misconduct. This is not only a matter of how employees feel; it is also a matter of how well the company performs and how much trouble it gets into.

Yet many leaders still feel they don't have time for company culture. They need results, they say, and they need them now! Behaviors and habits that influence the culture can develop slowly; the effects of a changing culture can also be very gradual. As with long-term health risks such as smoking or overeating, it can be hard to see the slow progress of dysfunction and cultural danger, yet the effects can be sudden and catastrophic. As the pace of business, innovation, and communication accelerates, companies can get into more trouble in less time than ever before—the corporate equivalent of the seemingly healthy person who suddenly has a heart attack. Ignoring longer-term cultural challenges in the name of short-term profits is an invitation for just that kind of blindsiding. A healthy corporate culture is not a luxury, not a nice-to-have, precisely because the risks can be very high and can come quickly. We have already seen in this chapter—and we see in the news every day—how, in dysfunctional cultures, smart people can end up making poor decisions, employees can be distracted from doing their jobs well, and risks can be taken that can put a company out of business or create a global crisis.

Organizations that do not understand how their culture affects behavior may not be able to sustain even their short-term goals. Several examples in later chapters show companies that are doing well enough but not nearly as well as they could be if the elements of their cultures weren't partially at odds with each other. Some of these companies are already feeling the pain; others probably will.

Many leaders who decide not to focus their attention on culture or simply never think of focusing on it do not know how much of a culture problem they already have. In Chapter Six, I relate the story of a global company that learns that one of its highest-performing units, a high-tech military contractor, was also one of its highest-risk units—a major misstep just waiting to happen. In my experience over the past twenty years, most leaders:

- Do not realize that their culture significantly hinders or supports performance and the implementation of strategies.
- Do not know whether their culture generates unacceptably high risks of unethical or illegal conduct.
- Do not see why a reorganization or acquisition is doomed to failure because leadership has failed to create a common culture, generating frustration that can lead to undesired behavior.

Why this blindness? Most leaders I've met are smart people. So why would they hesitate to do something beneficial for the company, especially if the steps are simple and logical?

Almost everyone trying to lose weight or stop smoking knows what he or she should do. Eat less and exercise more. Don't light up. If we try to understand why we don't do these simple, obvious things, we realize that there are behavioral roadblocks in our way—for example: "I've never had any self-control." A roadblock such as this requires awareness of the elements that need to be overcome and then of how those elements fit together. Changing behavior therefore requires a series of steps, each addressing a challenge in a way that opens the door to the next step. In this book, I will help you think about your organization's cultural risks and opportunities in terms of actionable items that you can gauge and manage.

BEHAVIOR AND CULTURE

Culture has an impact on performance, but you can't just calculate which kind of culture can make your organization high performing and then will that culture into place, as if it were a compensation plan or an operational directive. Even if your people agree that a certain culture is desirable—say, greater teamwork or more openness—they cannot simply stop acting one way and start acting another. As you will see, people act according to their personal values, but they are also powerfully influenced by the environment around them—in this case, the organizational culture—even to the point that the culture can modify their personal values.[9] As a result, you must influence behavior across your organization—and the good news is that you can. Culture is not only much more important than many leaders realize, but also much more actionable once you understand the key components and what keeps them working together for high performance and low ethical risk.

The first step toward removing the roadblocks that prevent your employees from doing their best is to understand what drives their behavior. In the companies I have worked with, the employees are generally good people who believe they are balancing their values, such as honesty and responsibility, with what is needed to get the job done. It turns out that like most other people, they can be pretty good at fooling themselves.

Although we would like to think that we are masters of our own decisions and actions, social norms and expectations significantly influence individual behavior. In the 1930s, Kurt Lewin, one of the pioneers of social psychology, conducted groundbreaking research on why people behave the way they do. Prior to Lewin, the prevailing theory had attributed a person's behavior to either his or her personality and character (nature) or circumstances (nurture); Lewin showed that it was both. We may therefore behave differently in different circumstances. We are neither completely good nor completely bad, and we do not always act in the most rational way. In the workplace, this means that any one of your employees at any time can decide to engage in activities that further the company's interests or their own interests. Of course, at the far ends of the spectrum are sociopaths, who are not influenced by their environment, and virtuous people, who do the right thing no matter what. But most of us are somewhere in the middle: we generally act in accordance with our personal values, but our sense of when and how to apply our values is influenced by the social norms in the workplace and the society around us. Achievement, for example, is a universally accepted personal value, but in some cultures, getting ahead at the expense of others' feelings is expected, while in others, the need to conform to group standards thwarts individual achievement. When making decisions, most employees instinctively search for a balance between two potentially opposing forces: their personal values—such as honesty, personal growth, and empathy toward others—and the social norms of their work environment. Research has shown that when these positions are not easily reconcilable, people are prone to put their personal values aside in deference to group norms or an authoritarian leader.

Recent research suggests that even our own sense of right and wrong is not as fixed as we would like to think. What is so important for leaders to understand is that our self-concept itself can change with the circumstances—in particular, with the organizational culture. Employees who feel honest can also feel pressured, influenced, or lured by the company's culture into doing things they did not set out to do, they are not proud of, or they would not do in other circumstances. In my experience, it is as if we have a number of mental switches that turn on under certain circumstances, dangerously shifting the emphasis of our decision making from the company's interest to forms of self-interest that can range from personal gain to sheer self-protection. The three most important of these switches are self-deception, rationalization, and disengagement:

○   *Self-deception: "I think it's okay to do this."* Sometimes self-deception allows us to think what we are doing is right, even though, in other circumstances (or if done by other people), we would know that it is wrong. Have you ever thought that maybe it isn't honest to accept the twenty-five-dollar bank error in your favor that has been part of Monopoly for three generations? If it never occurred to you, why not? Self-deception can even cloud our view of objective facts because we have such a vested interest in a particular decision. As I explain in Chapter Two, one reason that safety got away from BP in the 2010 Gulf of Mexico disaster was a type of self-deception that caused managers not to see risks right in front of them.

○   *Rationalization: "I know it's wrong, but I have a good reason for doing it."* Under pressure to meet short-term goals, the right thing to do can seem wrong and the wrong thing can seem right. For audit employees at the ill-fated telecommunications company WorldCom, for example, rationalizing misdeeds was justified when members of the audit team allowed themselves to be convinced that what they were doing was essential for saving the company. Once this switch is flipped, flipping it back is hard.

○   *Disengagement: "I know there's something wrong here, but it's not my problem"* or, *"Why should I bother trying to help? They won't listen to what I say or appreciate what I do."* Traditional rewards and punishments—raises and promotions or the denial of those things—can distort the more powerful intrinsic motivations of helping customers, helping one's team, or doing a job one can be proud of. (This is a particular problem for knowledge workers who seek satisfaction from their creative work above and beyond their paychecks.) Once employees are making a sufficient living, giving them a sense of accomplishment and purpose does more than financial rewards or punishments to motivate them to do their best. In fact, traditional methods of reward can sometimes be counterproductive. And for all kinds of employees, management that is (or seems) too busy to listen or even say hello is in fact a serious risk factor, flipping the switch so that employees' natural impulse to contribute to the company's success is cut off; instead, it seems right not to bother.

As the behavioral sciences reveal more about how we think and act, you need to understand how your organization's environment—its culture—influences that behavior.

ELEMENTS OF CULTURE

If the environment has an impact on your people's behavior, you need to control the environment. You can do this with a model that allows you to manage key levers and influencers to get the results you seek.

Do you know whether your organization's culture is a positive driver of performance or a roadblock? Do you know what kind of culture your organization needs in order to achieve its business objectives? A desired culture will not just reveal itself. You need to know which buttons to push, that is, which actions and directives will generate a high-performance culture. To be able to use your company's culture as a tool, you need to see how the elements of that culture are either working with or against each other. You need to see culture as dynamic and to know how to transform it from a negative influence on behavior to a positive influence on behavior. You need a model of culture that adds measurable parameters to the broad definition of "how we do things around here."

Let's start with the three core elements that define culture: the organization's mission and goals, principles and beliefs, and standards of behavior (Figure 1.1).

Figure 1.1   The Three Elements of Culture

Every organization has these elements, and its people can sense—even if they cannot articulate—whether each of these has its own internal consistency and whether they work together or get in each other's way. Are the organization's goals consistent with employees' individual goals? Are the official standards of behavior consistent with social norms? Are individual employee's principles and beliefs supported by the organization? These three elements are categories; what exactly is in them—which goals, which principles, which standards of which behavior—is something you will need to catalogue in order to create a more productive culture.

Each of these elements of culture has a relationship with the other two, but these relationships may be boosting performance and keeping a lid on risk or may be undermining performance and creating risk. You therefore need to align your organization's mission and goals, its principles and beliefs, and its standards of behavior to create a high-performing and well-behaving corporate culture. As you will see, when each of these three elements has its own internal coherence and is in alignment with the other two elements, employees at all levels feel engaged, committed, and free to work to their full capabilities. Performance is high, strategies are well executed, blunders are avoided or well handled, and lessons are learned. By contrast, in companies where these elements are internally inconsistent and are not well aligned—that is, they are working against one another—employees feel frustrated, disengaged, and reluctant (or even afraid) to raise issues. Performance is less than it could have been, strategies founder or are not carried out as well as they could have been, blunders are made and then mishandled so that they get even worse, and the same blunders are repeated.

Let's take a look at each of these elements of culture.

Mission and Goals: What Do We Strive For?

Goals influence behavior. Leaders and employees are compensated and rewarded for meeting targets and objectives. Goals include broad strategic objectives and individual objectives; the latter can include more subtle personal objectives such as getting ahead or just keeping your job. Employees at any level must ask themselves whether the goals they are pursuing conflict with their personal values and whether they have the time, ability, and resources to meet their personal goals as well as their assigned goals. If the answer to either question is no, the company's effectiveness decreases and the ethical risks increase.

Most employees have multiple goals, some of which can seem contradictory, counterproductive, impossible, or thwarted by the same management that demands them. The culture—how we do things around here—dictates which goals come first and what gets in the way. For example, many companies, including J&J, have a tension between getting product to market and ensuring quality. A healthy culture doesn't make that tension go away; it creates the means for that tension to be resolved in accordance with the company's and employees' values. A healthy culture creates a consistent way of addressing the issues so that they don't create crises every time the pressure gets high.

Some goals are visionary, inspiring employees' commitment and serving as a beacon around which the multitude of processes and procedures can come together. For example, the Timberland Company, the boot manufacturer known for its corporate responsibility and its outdoor apparel, has a business goal of becoming the number-one outdoor brand in the world. Its approach is to get there by keeping its business goals consistent with its values. It states on its Web site: "Our passion for the outdoors and responsibility to our stakeholders demand that we address one of the most pressing environmental issues of our time—climate change. Timberland aims to be part of the solution by reducing our energy demand, as well as procuring and investing in renewable energy and working with our partners to do the same."[10]

However, even visionary companies also have pragmatic business goals, such as expanding its market presence in Asia by 10 percent or reducing expenses across the board by 5 percent. Such goals may be essential to the organization's success, but it still needs to connect them to the workforce. Does each employee know how he or she fits into the overall picture? How can the organization frame its goals so that employees feel engaged?

Organizations whose employees can each put his or her whole heart into meeting the broader goals are the most likely to succeed. Each employee's goals are in alignment with the organization's goals. The challenges—and therefore the frustrations that create roadblocks— come when there is a disconnect between the organization's stated goals and either the goals or the principles of individual employees—in other words, when there is inconsistency within one of the basic elements of the company's culture or when two of those elements are misaligned.

Principles and Beliefs: What Do We Stand For?

A value is any principle, ideal, or belief that someone holds or adheres to when making decisions. As you will see in Chapter Three, each person embodies a myriad of values, and organizations embody the collective values of their people.

People naturally think of such things as honesty, cooperation, or excellence as values. When organizations announce their "values," they typically name such things as customer service, innovation, saving people's lives, or offering low prices. But values—as I am defining them—are not always positive or particularly uplifting. In some companies, bureaucracy is a value in the sense that it consistently guides how people make, or don't make, decisions, for example, going through delaying tactics rather than taking direct action to solve an immediate problem.

Individuals express their values through their personal behaviors; organizations express their values through their cultural behaviors. For example, if the decisions and actions taken by employees, from line workers to executives, are consistently aimed at maintaining or improving quality, then quality is a corporate value, a recognizable part of the culture. I would venture that fewer J&J employees would say they see quality in the culture now than would have said so fifteen years ago.

Some values count more than others. Core values are an individual's as well as the organization's deepest principles and beliefs, those the person or organization will be most reluctant to compromise or violate. Jim Collins calls these "essential and enduring tenets, not to be compromised for financial gain or short-term expediency."[11] Quality, for example, is—or at least was—a core value at J&J.

Ultimately principles and beliefs are answers to the critical question: Other than making money, why is this company in business? What does it stand for? Employees can and will measure whether the organization's goals and actions are consistent with its principles and with their own principles.

Standards of Behavior: How Do We Do What We Do?

Standards are the stated rules and operating procedures found in every organization—how to carry out tasks and procedures and how not to. These standards are found in written codes of conduct and operating manuals and taught formally in training programs and informally on the job.

Then there are the unwritten rules—the social norms—defining how the organization really operates and how people really behave—what's acceptable and what isn't. New employees pick up the social norms from more experienced coworkers. The gaps your people experience between expected behavior and how they and their coworkers really behave are key shapers of their culture. Understanding those gaps will help you see where there are or could be negative behaviors and how best to prevent them.

For example, no one at J&J's McNeil division would have instructed any employee to violate the Credo or any of the quality procedures or standards. No one wanted inferior or dangerous products to hit the shelves. The stated policies did not change. But as people grappled with tough production deadlines, contrary social norms such as, "Don't ask too many questions" or "We're not stopping any shipment without proof of a defect," crept into the culture. Employees and managers became less certain about which standards should prevail: the official behavior of the Credo or the real-life behavior guided by these new social norms.

Changes intended for a particular purpose can have unintended effects on an organization's social norms. For example, there were no wholesale layoffs in quality staff at McNeil. But other changes made it less likely that production deadlines would be challenged on quality grounds. Higher-paid, more experienced quality staff were laid off and replaced by employees with far less experience. The company thus lost not only some of the technical expertise required to maintain quality, but also much of the organizational memory of the 1982 Tylenol crisis—when seven people died from Tylenol that had been laced with cyanide—and what it had taken to survive it. Losing that collective memory weakened the strong social norm of putting quality before everything else. Furthermore, some of these younger employees were contractors, who felt themselves to be in no position to challenge their managers over quality. As a result, a high-pressure boss was less likely to be challenged.

This three-element model of culture has evolved from over twenty years of working with organizations and synthesizing the research done by business thought leaders such as Jim Collins, Robert Kaplan, and David Norton. Business strategist Jim Collins's extensive research on what makes companies great has focused on the relationships between an organization's core values and the obstacles that keep people from living those values.[12] These obstacles can be policies and practices—or, in my terms, standards of behavior—that run contrary to the organization's principles and beliefs. Going further, Collins looked at the linkage between an organization's principles and beliefs and its business objectives or goals. Successful companies understand the relationships between these elements and use them to ensure that their actions are consistent with their vision.

Robert Kaplan and David Norton looked at how organizations can better manage their intangible assets to achieve competitive advantage.[13] They found that successful companies have a culture in which people understand the relationships between the organization's core values (principles and beliefs), its strategy (mission and goals), and the implementation of that strategy (standards of behavior).

ALIGNMENT OF CULTURE

For thirty years, business scholars and consultants have marveled at the way J&J applied its principles in handling the 1982 Tylenol crisis. Under James Burke's leadership, J&J immediately pulled Tylenol—the brand that had been poisoned—from the shelves worldwide, even before the Food and Drug Administration or the Federal Bureau of Investigation could act. J&J took great pains to show the world that it was doing everything it could to protect the public's safety, not its own bottom line. The recall cost J&J an estimated $100 million, but the company's reputation was preserved and the Tylenol brand recovered.

Although McNeil Consumer Healthcare was only one of over two hundred companies within J&J, it was able to function quite autonomously at the time and had its own special culture with a very closely knit feeling among employees. The quality group was known to have an attitude of moral superiority. Quality was king, and quality managers had the authority to stop the production line if there were any doubts about product integrity. In this environment, the principles and beliefs that employees held dear—the primacy of quality, care for the people who relied on J&J products for their well-being—were reflected in the actions of the organization. Employees felt good about themselves because they could bring their values to work and would not have to compromise them.

That had all changed by 2005 when a sample from a batch of more than 1 million bottles of aspirin failed to dissolve according to specifications. Quality engineers, following procedures that were still on the books, blocked the product from being shipped. This time, however, the reaction was quite different. The quality manager called the quality engineers into his office and insisted there was no reason for this batch to fail. Afraid of losing their jobs, they devised new quality tests that ensured the defective pills would pass.

That significant values gaps had emerged was clear. The desire to do the right thing and the need to keep one's job had not been in conflict before. The stated principles and beliefs of the Credo were being challenged by the less glamorous goal of making the quarter-end numbers. McNeil managers were also quite upset with Colleen Goggins, who ran McNeil after it absorbed Pfizer's consumer products division. Her micromanagement, aimed at reducing costs to meet merger targets, undermined the sense of local accountability that had been a hallmark of McNeil's quality-driven culture. As you will see, this type of gap between what employees feel is right and what they can actually do affects performance by thwarting commitment and engagement.

Why couldn't J&J come through its business challenges without multiple recalls and a congressional investigation? There doesn't seem to be any real smoking gun in the form of particular policies or actions that would lead to such trouble. There is no reason to suspect Goggins of deliberately shipping faulty products. Instead, there were small actions that cumulatively altered employees' attitudes and actions. In *Good to Great,* Jim Collins talks about the flywheel, the gradual accumulation of small individual actions that eventually effect change. His research showed that in successful organizations, people feel that their day-to-day activities are serving a greater good (such as making people's lives better) consistent with the organization's goals (profit and growth). When people feel that they are part of a team and take pride in its accomplishments, they tend to do what it takes for that team to succeed.[14] In contrast, some of the actions J&J took as part of its merger with Pfizer—such as the cost cutting in production—generated a culture that led to subsequent quality problems. When enough small pebbles are dropped into a pond, the ripples can have a surprising impact. The trick—something most business leaders just don't know how to think about yet—is to understand which pebbles are having a negative impact and which will have a positive impact.

The sense of alignment that Collins observes between what employees are doing and what they most hope to accomplish comes about when the company's principles, goals, and standards support one another. For example, clear goals make it easier for employees to know which standards apply. This frees them to bring their values to work, which helps the company achieve its goals—a virtuous cycle. Employees share the organization's goals and are motivated by them. Their day-to-day work routines help them reach their goals while helping the company reach its goals. This had clearly been the case at J&J in the days of Jim Burke; when speed or profit conflicted with quality, the Credo made it clear which was to take priority. The result was not corporate weakness or paralysis but great corporate vitality and success.

THE POWER VALUES

How can an organization align its culture to achieve maximum performance yet avoid inappropriate behavior such as cheating on a compliance exam or rewriting the quality rules to get defective product out the door? The key is in the influential behaviors embodied in certain critical values. By definition, all values guide behavior—for better or worse—but in the context of a business, some values guide behavior in particularly productive ways. Perhaps this is why the work of legendary psychologist Abraham Maslow still has so much to offer. The more we appreciate how great a role psychology plays in decision making, the more we need a way to look at subconscious influences on behavior—such as values—in language that meets the needs of pragmatic business leaders.

Maslow's famous hierarchy of human needs presents our subconscious motivations in terms of individual and collective levels of awareness that organizations can use as a tool. One key level of awareness in a model I use that is based on Maslow is a communal desire to feel attached to others and connected to something bigger than ourselves. My work with companies over the past twenty years has shown me that three of the values found at this communal level of awareness—integrity, commitment, and transparency—stand out for their roles in fostering identification and community. I call these the *power values* because they can influence specific behaviors that will have a positive influence on an organization's culture (Figure 1.2). These are the behaviors that will push and nudge the organization's goals, principles, and standards into alignment. The power values do not give you power over other people, but they give you the power to bring out the best in people. By focusing on the specific behaviors that make up integrity, commitment, and transparency, you can transform the

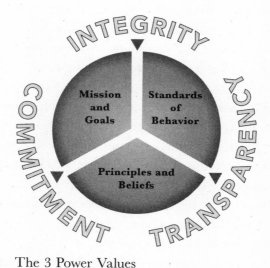

Figure 1.2 The 3 Power Values

negative behaviors that impede effective performance into positive behaviors that support effective performance. Company culture becomes a measurable and manageable tool with which to rev up performance and reduce risk.

To avoid confusion, let me point out that the power values, despite the name I have given them, do not necessarily have to be your personal—or your company's—core values. How can this be? An example from outside the business world may be helpful. In 2011 the United States witnessed several discouraging clashes of will in the Congress. Representatives with very different sets of core values were unable to reach agreement on serious policy matters affecting the federal debt. For some representatives, their core values embodied principles of self-reliance; for others, their core values reflected principles of collective responsibility. However, the organization—in this case, the U.S. Congress—needed an enabling value in order to achieve alignment: the value of compromise. In politics, then, compromise, though perhaps not a core value of any one member, is a power value of the institution.

The 3 power values are powerful catalysts for another reason: they are already the personal values that your employees commonly hold. When the power values are highly visible in an organization, they clarify its intentions and give employees a unifying sense of purpose and direction. Employees who share their principles, goals, and outlook—the essence of the power values—can let their guard down a bit. They can trust that they will be understood, that there will be fewer booby traps, and that their leaders and coworkers will generally act in a predictable way, consistent with their shared values.

In my work, I have seen that organizations whose employees live these power values are marked by dedication, openness, and personal responsibility. Employees in those companies take the initiative to ensure that their company can achieve its goals in the short term without sacrificing long-run sustainability. The employees of Beth Israel Deaconess Medical Center in Boston are a perfect example. Several years ago, the hospital's CEO at the time, Paul Levy, was up-front in telling employees that potential cuts were looming, but he gave them the opportunity to help leadership prioritize and develop less expensive approaches. Engaged employees responded with a wealth of innovations.

As you come to understand the unique challenges of living up to your employees' expectations of integrity, commitment, and transparency and begin to see where unaligned principles, goals, and standards are creating friction and risk, you can identify the linchpin behaviors that will have a cascading impact throughout your organization. But first you must be aware of the specific relationships among goals, principles, and standards. You must find a way to align your company's standards with its goals, its principles with its goals, and its standards with its principles. The power values—commitment, integrity, and transparency—will be your tools.

Integrity Links Standards and Goals

The word *integrity* is more than a synonym for *honesty*. It refers to integration—making the parts of something into a whole. For me, integrity is a matter of combining one's various words and actions into a harmonious whole. People who act with integrity are doing what they said they would do, living their values through their actions. An organization that is acting with integrity is consistent and predictable in its business processes: what happens today will happen tomorrow. When employees see their managers act consistently and predictably and procedures are seen as fair, stress levels are lower because there are fewer surprises and fewer crises. For example, as long as jobs are assigned and success is rewarded fairly, employees can afford to trust their leaders and the organization and do not feel they need to connive just to get a fair shake. If they do not need to connive, they will not subsequently need to rationalize their conniving or deceive themselves that their conniving is honest—the slippery slope is avoided.

Thus, integrity links an organization's goals—what we say we're going to do—with its standards—what we actually do. This determination to walk the talk is one foundation of a healthy company culture.

Commitment Links Principles and Goals

Have you ever been at a company where everyone seemed passionate about the work they were doing as well as the work the organization was doing? There is electricity in the air. Engaged and committed employees will go the extra mile for their organization's success because its goals are their goals. The key to fostering that kind of commitment is to ensure that employees feel that bringing their personal values to work is not a risk. Rather, it is part of the culture.

Retail chains typically have a big problem with employee commitment; most have high turnover and spend a fortune hiring and training new personnel. So any successful effort to increase the engagement of hourly staff has a direct impact on the bottom line. Not too long ago, apparel giant The Gap, along with other merchants, partnered with the nonprofit organization Project RED to raise awareness of the need to stamp out AIDS in Africa and to raise money with which to do it. For The Gap, this was a good way to align its corporate principles with its business decision to source merchandise from Africa. At selected stores, one sales associate was designated to be the "RED leader," responsible for telling customers and other employees about the program. Project RED sent representatives incognito to see how committed certain stores were to the program and how well their sales associates had been trained. One such representative was later in tears as she told a Gap senior executive about a RED leader who had not only memorized the information in her briefing packet but had also gone online to gather much more information about AIDS in Africa and what was being done about it. This young employee's principles were fully aligned with The Gap's business goals, and she was clearly passionate about the project, proud of the responsibility she had been given, and committed to her company for giving her such an opportunity.

An organization's goals are not always consistent with its employees' principles, to put it mildly. I once had a boss who did not care what his sales team sold or how we sold it as long as we met our numbers. My goal, however, was to build relationships and develop creative tools to meet my customers' needs. I did my job, but I was not committed to it and left as soon as I could for a position in which I could put more of my heart into my work.

Long-time J&J employees remember their passion for the company's mission. The Credo bonded employees around a common purpose. The subsequent disconnect between the short-term profit goals and the legacy values—and the resulting string of recalls and scandals—has undermined that commitment. *Fortune* magazine reporter Mina Kimes, in an investigation of the challenges facing J&J, noted that the team that tested the production lines had come to be called "EZ Pass," named after the electronic toll collection system used to speed drivers through tollbooths. In one instance, an engineering flaw on a production line made it difficult to clean liquid-medicine bottles. Rather than find a way to fix the problem, the team tried to eliminate that check from the test.[15] They could hardly have felt personally committed to such a goal. They couldn't even have felt it was an unpleasant but necessary step toward a goal they could feel committed to. The fact that they did it anyway shows how misaligned the elements of J&J's culture had become.

Transparency Links Standards and Principles

Transparency is your organization's insistence that the truth be heard, even when it is hard, and that it be clear what behaviors are expected and whether those behaviors are consistent with the organization's principles. Can your people be open and honest with each other? Do they have full access to the information they want or only to the information someone else is willing to provide? Transparency can go a long way toward preventing disappointing performance and unethical behavior, especially when it saves people from their own self-deception, rationalization, or disengagement.

But transparency is an issue only when the information one seeks is hard for the other person to deliver or when the information one wants to convey will be hard for the other person to hear. Transparency therefore embodies the value of honesty. Employees at all levels must be determined to act according to their principles. The company's culture can help by establishing a norm of speaking up, particularly if leaders make a habit of speaking up even when it is embarrassing or difficult for them to do so. To the extent that people's discomfort is fear, establishing a norm of respect and open communication lowers the hurdle, particularly if leaders make a point of tolerating speaking up even when the news is hard for them to take.

How does an organization go about creating a culture in which difficult issues can be discussed? The first step is to understand that these challenges exist because of a gap between what employees believe (their principles) and how they act (the standards, or social norms). Just as integrity is doing what you say you will do, consistently linking your actions to your goals (or the company's goals), transparency is being true to yourself, consistently linking your actions to your principles. Transparency thus encourages honesty, which, according to surveys, is the prevailing personal value of employees all over the world. More than any other value, employees expect honesty of themselves and of those with whom they work. I am struck by how often managers tell me that the thing they most wish from their people is to be told when something is wrong.

When standards—how we do things—and principles—why we do them—are aligned, employees and managers don't fear raising difficult issues or admitting mistakes. For example, an engineer who raises a concern about product quality is given a chance to be heard and to help resolve the issue. Even if it turns out she was wrong, she is respected for having the company's welfare at heart. The incident becomes an opportunity to learn, itself a form of respect: "We're convinced it's worth sticking with you through some mistakes because we see your potential."

The manner in which J&J handled the 1982 Tylenol crisis has always been the model of transparency—an organization acting in a manner consistent with its principles. J&J immediately pulled the product from the shelves without regard to cost or public embarrassment. It did not obfuscate or disclaim responsibility on the grounds that no employee had done the tampering. Although the FBI felt that pulling Tylenol nationwide would be a capitulation to the terrorist who had poisoned the product—something like paying ransom—J&J did it anyway because the Credo demanded it. J&J phone banks answered questions from consumers and from the media; they would even get back to reporters if answers to their questions weren't immediately available.

In repeated interviews, Jim Burke said that J&J's Credo made it easy for him and his team to know exactly what to do. The Credo states that J&J's "first responsibility is to the doctors, nurses, and patients, to the mothers and all the others who use our products and services." One observer has noted that J&J's capacity for such transparency in 1982 may have been due in part to an extraordinary exercise in transparency that Burke conducted in 1976. Sensing that the Credo was losing some its power, he met with his top managers for the express purpose of hearing out any criticism of it. The result seems to have been a rededication to the Credo, which helped save the day in 1982.

In stark contrast, McNeil leadership under Colleen Goggins has been described as evasive. Instead of taking responsibility for the unethical phantom recall, Goggins stated in her testimony before Congress, "Unfortunately, there has been some confusion in the media with respect to this recall," stressing that the recalled drugs had not been shown to cause illness. Donald Riker, a consultant to over-the-counter drug companies, said, "At every step in this process J&J has not been transparent. Every bit of information is cagey, secretive, and micromanaged."[16]

Putting the Pieces Together

Integrity, commitment, and transparency do not operate independently; each depends on the others. But an organization should probably not try to address all three power values at once. Rather, it needs to know which value is the weakest link requiring the most immediate intervention. By understanding how the elements of the company's culture affect each other, you can avoid unintended consequences and will be much more likely to create a virtuous cycle, with positive actions within one element of the culture promoting positive changes in the other two elements to create a positive feedback loop.

For example, the critical need for Johnson & Johnson is to restore transparency. Employees are not raising issues about quality in part because leaders have not demanded transparency of themselves and others. Burke succeeded in the 1982 Tylenol crisis because he was open to the world about what he knew and what he did not know. Restoring transparency—making it possible again for J&J employees to safely raise issues and to challenge whether decisions are consistent with the organization's core values—would begin to restore integrity and therefore a strong sense of commitment. A sense of commitment would make employees more likely to speak up about potential problems; they wouldn't want to see their company get into any trouble.

For other organizations, restoring or improving integrity is the proper starting point in removing a performance roadblock. Bureaucracy, inconsistency, and confusion are often among the top ten values reported in cultural assessments of major organizations. These negative values can create a vicious cycle. For example, when confusion about processes and procedures generates inefficiencies, frustrated employees develop a culture of blame in which they cannot communicate effectively. This lack of transparency leaves people feeling left out of the information loop, which erodes commitment and engagement. Frustrated employees may also conclude that there is no point in trying to do their best; this lack of commitment feeds on the lack of integrity, making it harder to improve the ineffective systems. And frustrated employees may be driven to cut corners and bend the rules just to get something done, putting their companies, and perhaps their coworkers and customers, at risk.

For yet other organizations, commitment is the starting point. After a merger, for example, employees often lose their sense of identification with and attachment to the company. This erodes their willingness to walk the new talk, undermining integrity, while at the same time inhibiting their desire to be open and honest with the new leadership, undermining transparency.

The 3 Power Values will show you how to identify those linchpin behaviors that help generate the positive feedback loops that drive high performance.

Behavior Roadblocks

We don't see . . . two or three people sitting there at a table
. . . giving up safety for cost . . . Workers on the rigs and on
shore want to be efficient and they don't want to waste money,
but they don't want their buddies to get killed either. I don't
believe people sit there and say, "This is really dangerous, but
the guys in London will make more money, so let's go ahead."
It's more complicated than that.

Fred Bartlitt, lead counsel, briefing of
National Commission of the BP Deepwater Horizon
Oil Spill and Offshore Drilling, November 9, 2010

Did anyone investigating the 2010 BP oil disaster in the Gulf of
Mexico really expect to find a smoking-gun document proving
that senior leaders intentionally traded off safety for profit? And yet few
people were satisfied in June 2010 when BP's CEO, Tony Hayward,
said that the industry had not anticipated an accident in which all the
fail-safe mechanisms failed. Had BP really never considered such a
possibility? If so, what were the blinders that BP's leaders and managers
allowed themselves to wear so as not to see risks that seemed obvious
to everyone else?

The starting point of any effort to create a high-performance culture is to determine the most basic influences of behavior. At the very core of the performance challenges facing organizations are behavior roadblocks intrinsic to our human nature. Being aware of them is the first step in effectively managing them. Unless you can create an environment that makes people feel safe acting altruistically, they are likely to fall back on protective and self-focused behaviors.

A look at how BP leaders approached safety provides insight into how those behavior roadblocks can cloud decision making. A deeper understanding of why neither Bartlitt's statement nor Hayward's is satisfactory offers a glimpse of the deep influence of organizational culture on how individual employees act, helping shape biases and decisions that may have consequences for millions of people.

I have worked with a number of global companies that handle hazardous materials, so I find it easy to believe that safety was on the mind of every manager at BP and that their expressed concern for protecting colleagues and the environment was real. However, at BP, as at most other companies, financial performance seemed to be the only metric that mattered. Managers may have a sincere concern for safety, but they are rewarded for meeting financial goals. The goals of safety and profit should not have to be incompatible, but it often feels as if they are.

At the time of the April 2010 explosion, BP's Macondo project in the Gulf of Mexico was more than a month behind schedule and more than $40 million over budget. Field managers were under tremendous pressure to get the well plugged so the $1-million-per-day Deepwater Horizon drilling platform could move on to other fields. Local observers of the oil industry knew what was going on. There was a sense of urgency in the air. The issue wasn't whether BP employees made a conscious trade-off between safety and dollars, but whether the way in which they handled the pressure made such a trade-off inevitable.[1] While the pressure on a company at a particular time may be largely out of its control, the way it handles that pressure is largely a matter of the culture it has cultivated over the years, deliberately or inadvertently.

Of course, financial pressure doesn't mean safety was not important to BP. In fact, the irony is that Tony Hayward came on board in 2007 as a champion of safety. Following in the footsteps of the larger-than-life Lord John Browne, Hayward conveyed a more pragmatic management style, firmly committing to the board of directors that he would focus on safety. Hayward felt confident he could balance the urgent need to make significant safety reforms while increasing profits to catch up with BP's primary rival, Shell. Hayward even sent his managers to a six-week "Operations Academy" at MIT, where they learned to balance risk with their business objectives.[2]

But the company seems to have developed a culture that caused many of its executives and managers to flip the self-deception switch mentioned in Chapter One. Leaders at BP believed that they were effectively managing safety, but they seem also to have been kidding themselves. Peter Elkind, an investigative reporter for *Fortune*, discovered that BP had such comprehensive safety regulations that an employee could not even carry a cup of coffee without a lid, yet there was no standard protocol for something as critical as the negative-pressure test that led to the explosion.[3] BP was addressing field safety issues that affected workers, such as the need to wear protective gear and to have safety procedures in place. But it failed to execute corporate-wide safety-risk strategies that addressed how it managed risks in terms of the procedures and processes to implement at various stages of drilling. These issues had been well known before the April 2010 disaster. In 2007, BP had published the findings of the blue-ribbon panel it had created to study the 2005 explosion at its Texas City refinery, which had killed fifteen workers.[4] The report stated that BP had not instilled a common unified safety culture among its U.S. refineries: "The Panel found instances of a lack of operating discipline, toleration of serious deviations from safe operating practices, and apparent complacency toward serious process-safety risks at each refinery."

Why was a safety-minded CEO like Tony Hayward unable to manage his company's obvious safety risks? Why couldn't BP instill a safety culture even after its own damning reports expressed the urgent need to do so? Why weren't senior leaders able to demand the necessary behaviors on the part of managers and field personnel? Why weren't employees who felt their own safety was in danger empowered to speak up?

Part of the answer is that in addressing the pressing questions of how to keep their company competitive—or even out of trouble—business leaders focus most of their attention on strategy and analytical solutions to improve processes. They give too little attention to the execution of strategy and even less to finding out why people fail to implement strategic directives. Perhaps there is an assumption that smart managers in the field will figure out how to balance implementation of broad safety directives with aggressive production goals and that if the effort fails, there must be some external factor or some particularly ill-intentioned employee to blame. In any case, BP focused its efforts on developing safety strategies without looking deeply enough into the roadblocks that would keep those strategies from being effectively implemented.

WE'RE NOT WHO WE THINK WE ARE

In order to understand why BP's best intentions went astray, we need to ask a couple of fundamental questions: Why do people, even with the best of intentions, fall short in acting consistently with their values? What holds us back? Why are we so vulnerable to external influences, and why don't we know how to manage the conflicts within our heads? The power values of commitment, integrity, and transparency can help organizations better manage people precisely because these are the values that serve as counterweights to our human tendencies to go off-track. But before we learn more about how the power values guide behavior, we need to see what research is revealing about how we think and act.

Imagine you and your colleagues are developing a safety strategy for your organization. You assume that leaders throughout the company think the way you do and sincerely recognize the importance of workplace safety. You also recognize that although safety is vitally important to the leadership team, so are the values of achievement and recognition, especially because you and your team are charged with meeting aggressive business objectives. In order to find a balance between maintaining reasonable safety standards and making a profit, you and your colleagues will probably come to a decision as to which safety risks are acceptable and which are not. Neither you nor anyone else in the company would ever make a conscious decision to violate safety standards in the name of profit. Yet even with this commitment in mind, could you be absolutely certain that you are not susceptible to influences that would cause you to violate your principles? Is there any possibility that you would compromise a safety standard? No? Don't be so sure.

It turns out that we have less control of our needs and motives than we like to think. As researchers go deeper into the human psyche, we are learning that much of what frames our decisions is not based on a rational view of the choices before us, but rather on deeper innate needs that subconsciously influence how we see the world and that even filter what we see. So although you would like to think that managers and employees in the field will rationally execute your company's objective strategies, subjective and unpredictable aspects of human nature cloud decision making. Because many aspects of these unconscious motivations originate in external factors such as culture, you need to be aware of how we all process the external stimuli that drive our actions. Otherwise you cannot hope to influence that behavior to help your organization meet its goals.

The first reality check is to come to grips with the fact that despite our best intentions, we do not always act according to our own values, even when we think we are doing so. Leaders such as Tony Hayward at BP and Colleen Goggins at Johnson & Johnson may be demonized in the press as evil people, but it is not at all likely that they are sociopaths. Probably they consider themselves to be as values driven and upstanding as anyone else—and maybe they are. The hard reality is that although we all have values that define us and guide our decision making, we also choose to apply those values selectively. Sometimes the decision to apply—or not apply—our values is a conscious one, and sometimes it is made in our subconscious.

Here's a little experiment to show how we all selectively apply our values. Imagine you are having lunch at a local diner where college students wait the tables. During one busy lunch hour, your waiter gives you an extra ten dollars in change. Do you keep the money as a lucky opportunity that came your way, or do you return it? Most people would return it. They know that the waiter may be responsible for balancing his till, so keeping the money would seem like taking it out of his pocket. Technically it might not be stealing, but to most people, it wouldn't seem right.

Now what happens if you open your monthly mobile phone bill and see that your carrier made a ten-dollar mistake in your favor? Do you report it? Although the small percentage of perfect angels who do the right thing in all circumstances will make the effort to report the mistake, the vast majority of us would not bother. Why not? You still have ten dollars at the expense of another, yet when I pose this question to audiences, they have no trouble coming up with reasons to keep the money:

- "They wouldn't even know what to do if I called them to report it. It's not worth their effort to take the money back."
- "Do you know how many times that @%&! company has ripped me off before?! This ten dollars is just a drop in the bucket compared to what they owe me!"
- "Do you know how much time it would take for me to call them and try to fix the mistake? Certainly more than ten dollars of my time."

Although each of these reasons may seem credible, the question is whether we are honestly applying our values or rationalizing our decision to keep the money. To know for sure, we would have to have our heads examined, although there are of course cognitive limitations on our ability to see the moral implications of our actions. Recent research shows that in spite of our own sense of morals and awareness of the right thing to do, we are also vulnerable to other neurological and psychological influences that complicate our decision making.

But does that mean that we just can't help it? Kurt Lewin's insight that behavior is shaped not only by personality but also by the environment may seem obvious to us today. We are comfortable with the concept that in addition to the neurological and psychological influences at work inside our own heads, external influences, such as work pressures and goals, can cloud the ethical aspect of our decisions. Yet business leaders have been slow to integrate this thinking into how they run their companies. The conventional wisdom used to be that external influences, such as intimidation or extreme pressure, could push good people over the edge and cause them to violate—reluctantly but consciously—the company's and their own standards. Now we are learning that external pressures can actually keep people from even seeing that what they are doing is wrong in the first place. So saying "I couldn't help it" may not be an excuse, but we cannot ignore the behavior motivators that cause us to say and feel that.

As a leader, you may be asking if you really have to probe into the human psyche like this in order to meet your business goals. You may feel that creating a high-performing corporate culture should not oblige you to become a corporate psychologist. But if you are going to create an action plan that will motivate behavior change, such as a companywide safety reform, that plan needs to take into account the fundamental cognitive biases that affect decision making—the three mental switches that turn on self-deception, rationalization, and disengagement. Thinking of them as switches reminds us that we may have an innate capacity for, say, self-deception, but this capacity is brought to bear in some circumstances and not in others. Those circumstances are, in Lewin's terms, our environment, and, in this book's terms, the organizational culture—its mix of principles, goals, and standards.

Because of the power these switches have to cloud the decision making of intelligent managers and employees, you need to develop strategies to mitigate the risks they create.

Self-Deception

Self-deception is a risk whenever we are unaware of the processes that lead us to form our opinions, which—truth to tell—is most of the time. We are really good at creating our own realities—past, present, and future. We tend to have false memories of past actions, thinking, "I've always acted virtuously," even if we have not, and we are poor predictors of how we will behave in the future, thinking, "I always will act virtuously," even though the statement is based more on hope than likelihood. As for the present, you tell yourself, "I think it's okay to do this," but really it isn't. You might not even be aware that you are acting against your own values or creating risk for yourself or for others. We shape our reality in favor of self-serving perceptions that make us feel good about ourselves.[5]

Behavioral economist Dan Ariely's recent research has shown that although we all like to think of ourselves as honest people who act nobly according to our values, most people behave dishonestly up to the point where they can no longer delude themselves that they are acting properly.[6] According to Ariely, we are all inclined to cheat, but just a little bit. Most people, even given the opportunity to cheat a lot, will not. We may not steal money from the petty cash drawer at the office, but we might take some pens home. Although we have our own sense of right and wrong, we have also internalized the social norms of our community. These norms are the benchmark against which we determine if we are acting properly. If we act against these norms, we do not feel good about ourselves—an important deterrent to negative behavior. We don't keep the ten-dollar overpayment from the college waiter in part because we won't feel good about ourselves if we do. But keeping the ten dollars from the mobile phone company is a different matter. Chances are you could tell your friends how you received some "payback" from the phone company and get nods of approval. But would your friends approve if you had decided not to give that ten dollars back to the waiter? We have such a strong desire to believe that we are doing the right thing that we develop blinders. Our ability to engage in self-deception causes us to think that what we are doing is acceptable.[7] In fact, sometimes we even create a special category in our minds for certain decisions to which our own values do not apply. For example, I have often heard managers explain to me that the tough (and questionable) actions they took were "business" decisions, not "ethics" decisions.

Psychologists have documented the power of a single goal to shape a whole series of small decisions that lead to undesired outcomes. For example, in the 1990s, Sears gave its auto repair mechanics a fixed sales goal of $147 per hour. Lo and behold, it wasn't long before customers began to be overcharged or sold unnecessary repairs. Many managers and leaders have the goal of being firm and focused in their decision making, which they take to be a requirement of good leadership. They can then convince themselves that coming to quick decisions is good, even if that decision is not well thought out. Over time they can succumb to a form of arrogance without actually feeling themselves to be particularly proud or superior. A safety manager might be thinking, *We've had no accidents or major incidents. Therefore we must be doing the right thing.*

This might have been what was going on at BP in 2010. Five years before the Deepwater Horizon disaster, BP had faced a potentially devastating loss. During Hurricane Dennis in 2005, the $1 billion Thunder Horse oil platform began listing precariously when a valve that had been installed backward caused the vessel to flood. An engineer who worked on the vessel said later that BP had rushed construction in order to show shareholders that it could meet production deadlines. The faulty valve installation was an avoidable error. The rig nearly sank, which would have caused a major oil spill. But it didn't. Yet subsequent investigative reports showed that this installation failure was not an anomaly.[8] According to analysts, BP was not taking its safety risks seriously enough in its quest for growth and revenue. Steve Arendt, a safety specialist assisting BP, said that "they were very arrogant and proud and in denial. It is possible they were fooled by their success."[9]

BP had created a culture in which many managers, not only a few, were unable to see risks in a clear and pragmatic way. Even after major investigations revealed significant safety lapses behind spills and injuries in Alaska and Texas, BP did not—or was not able to—change management practices in the field. Congressional investigations of the Deepwater Horizon disaster showed that before the blowout, BP repeatedly failed to use sufficient resources to stabilize the well and failed to run standard tests to determine if key procedures were working.

Hersh Shefrin, an expert in behavioral finance who has extensively studied BP, has identified four types of self-deception that color the way in which leaders look at risks:[10]

1. *Excessive optimism.* We sometimes look at the world through rose-colored glasses, overestimating the likelihood of favorable events and underestimating the likelihood of unfavorable events. A number of oil industry leaders said that the design of the Macondo well ignored many established industry standards and norms because BP didn't weigh the downside risks in the same way as other energy producers did.

2. *Overconfidence.* We can overestimate our own knowledge and ability, including the ability to assess the risks we face. This is a particularly acute risk for senior leaders as they become more and more isolated from the people in the organization who would tell them the truth and correct their inaccurate perceptions. For example, BP stated in its permit applications for the Macondo well in the Gulf that it could handle a leak of up to 250,000 barrels of oil per day. Given what actually happened, such a claim was clearly overconfident.

3. *Aversion to a sure loss.* We can tilt our decisions toward avoiding loss, even if it is not in our economic best interest to be so risk averse. The work of Amos Tversky and Nobel laureate Daniel Kahneman showed that avoiding loss is twice as powerful a motive as seeking gain.[11] For example, as the Deepwater Horizon project missed its

deadlines and went further and further over budget, taking greater risks to avoid even more certain financial losses started to seem more reasonable.

4. *Confirmation bias.* We regularly give too much credence to evidence that confirms our views and dismiss evidence that contradicts our views. You support a particular politician and can point out his good points. But your friend disagrees and points out that politician's obvious shortcomings. You can't really deny the facts, yet somehow your friend's facts don't sway you the way "your" facts do. As leaders, we tend to overvalue the successful outcome of a questionable action. If a poor decision turns out well, we rarely go back and analyze whether the organization got lucky or whether a significant risk really was adequately managed.

As managers wade through piles of information to make decisions, opportunities are always there to weight different information differently. No individual choice may be particularly wrongheaded or risky, yet they can add up to a disaster. Confirmation biases, for example, may keep managers from taking a broader view of the total risks posed in a complex operation, especially in an organization in which leaders make it known that they do not like hearing bad news.

These common tendencies toward self-deception become even more pronounced the higher up a person is on the corporate ladder. As we take on more responsibility and authority, we become vulnerable to a type of self-deception that psychologists call the "paradox of power." Researchers have found that people in positions of power—even good, empathetic, and sensitive people—begin to change. They can act like fools, causing the rest of us to ask, "Just what were those people [Bill Clinton, John Edwards, Eliot Spitzer, Herman Cain, Harry Stonecipher] thinking?" According to psychologist Dacher Keltner at the University of California, Berkeley, people in power become more likely than they previously would have been to take impulsive actions, such as flirting inappropriately. Keltner equated the feeling of power to a type of brain damage; the corner office can cause good people to lose their ability to be empathetic. Give good people power, and they might start acting like fools.[12]

Psychological studies have also shown that people in positions of authority become more isolated and therefore make decisions and treat others based on stereotypes and generalizations. Unfortunately, my experience with large organizations confirms much of this research. While the most senior leaders are often able to acknowledge and overcome these biases, those more junior in rank or age often are not. For example, not too long ago I worked with a global manufacturing and electronics corporation, which I'll call USZ. Corporate headquarters would send high-potential young executives out to the field to get a better understanding of operations. These managers from "corporate" were not popular in the field; hourly employees found them cold and aloof. They would walk through the plant with their heads in their spreadsheets and not even make eye contact with the operations staff who would say "hello" or "good morning." They were too focused on their strategy objectives to see the "human" in their human resources. I see this pattern in many companies. These managers did not think they were being rude and would never have claimed that their employees were not human beings deserving of ordinary politeness, yet they deceived themselves that they were acting decently.

A colleague once told me that inside one's head can be a very dangerous neighborhood because of our ability to create our own realities. That's exactly what the three mental switches do; understanding that process is a powerful means of ensuring that we make good decisions that don't leave others wondering, *What on earth was he thinking?*

Rationalization

While self-deception means not recognizing that you are engaged in inappropriate behavior, rationalization means that you know you are acting (or have acted) contrary to your values, but you feel you have reasons to justify what you are doing (or have done): "I know it's wrong, but there are good reasons why I did it." What causes us to feel and act this way?

Have you ever been in the position of weighing options, one of which has the best outcome but the highest risk? In taking the riskiest option, you may be compromising other values, such as integrity, safety, quality, or perhaps some longer-term benefit, in order to meet a short-term goal. In your head you have convinced yourself that this more aggressive course of action is necessary; you think it would be a shame—even irresponsible—to pass up the maximum benefit. In doing so, you may have underestimated the downside risks. But when you talk about it with a confidante, she gives you that look that says, *Are you crazy? What are you thinking?* Sometimes just being challenged by another person is enough to straighten out one's thinking.

In my work with major organizations, I have found that rationalization typically takes one of three paths:

- People know that what they are doing is wrong, but they think they have no choice. Some work in an environment in which winning at all costs is the only way to keep one's job. Others tell me that "family" is their number-one value, and they will do whatever it takes to keep their families financially secure.
- When people perceive they are being treated unfairly, they stop looking out for what is best for the organization and focus only on what is best for them. "I am entitled to take this action because I was unfairly passed over for a promotion, and I have not been adequately recognized or compensated for the work I have done."
- The peer pressure is too great: "Everyone else is doing this, and I'm not going to be seen as a loser."

Peer pressure can apply to companies as well as people. From 1999 to 2002, for example, as many as 43 percent of publicly traded companies backdated stock options for executives and managers: granting an option that was dated prior to the date on which it was actually granted. The beneficiary of the option would therefore able to obtain a higher profit because the "future" stock price was already known. At the time, options backdating was legal as long as it was properly expensed in the company's financial statements and properly disclosed to regulatory authorities. Yet the ethics of it was questionable from the start: if an option was given as an incentive to help increase the stock price, it seemed disingenuous to profit on an increase that had occurred before the option was granted. So how was it that so many well-known executives, such as Steve Jobs at Apple, engaged in such a questionable practice, especially if it was perceived as being unseemly, if not blatantly unethical, by the public?

The answer is surprisingly simple: everyone was doing it. An unethical social norm was working in a legal gray area. In a competitive culture such as Silicon Valley, the competition for the best benefits package was extreme. Everybody wanted to be recognized for his or her incredible managerial prowess, and nobody wanted to be left out of a significant upside financial benefit. Thanks to Silicon Valley's network of interlocking boards of directors, once one company began backdating options, many others followed. When a board member of a company that was already doing it with good results brought that idea to another company, it had greater legitimacy. Only when the Securities and Exchange Commission finally took public enforcement actions against those who were not legally disclosing their options did the reality of how this practice was seen by the public sink in.

It can be surprisingly easy to flip the switch that makes someone rationalize conformance to a group norm he or she would not previously have gone along with. As Solomon Asch found in his famous conformity experiments in the 1950s, participants were more than willing to make false statements so as not be the only one violating what appeared to be a group norm.[13] In the classic experiment, college students were invited to participate in a research study on visual acuity. The true participant was brought into a room full of other college students who were confederates with the researcher. The researcher presented charts showing a line and then four other lines of differing lengths. Each participant was asked to say which of the four choices matched the line on the chart. After several rounds, all of the confederates began giving the wrong answer. Typically the participant would become confused as to why everyone else in the room was giving an obviously incorrect answer. For a few rounds, the participant would stick to his or her guns and answer correctly, but eventually most participants would conform to the group falsehoods. Only 26 percent of the participants refused to conform to the group error and, in nearly 33 percent of all the rounds, the participant conformed.

At the core of rationalization is a series of unfulfilled needs linked to deep-seated anxieties or fears that challenge our otherwise good judgment. Because of these fears, we are incredibly focused—perhaps subconsciously—on meeting these needs. We might even be obsessed. There are three such needs in particular that matter most to business leaders:

1. *Need to succeed.* Have you ever met someone who is never satisfied with his material possessions? He may be very comfortable, even wealthy, but he always wants more. This need may be plain old greed, but it may also be linked to more deeply rooted anxieties about survival.

2. *Need to be liked.* There are other people who have such an insatiable need to be liked or to feel that they are part of a particular group that it clouds their objective reason. From David Myers at World-Com (whom we will meet later in this chapter) to Jérôme Kerviel at Société Générale, there are many examples of scandals that were driven at least in part by someone's fear of not being liked or not being included.

3. *Need for acceptance.* Many employees have an underlying anxiety or fear about their ranking in relation to their peers. An incredible focus on bolstering their self-esteem—by acquiring power, authority, status, or respect—can cloud their decision making. These over-achievers can never get enough recognition or praise to satisfy them.

One of the greatest challenges in regulating our own tendency to rationalize is that the line between rationality and rationalization is rarely clear. What starts out as an attempt to meet an aggressive goal can lead to confusion as we try to manage a quickly unraveling situation. In such distress, we may be willing to grasp at any source of authority or precedent that can justify our actions. During the most notorious financial scandals of the previous decade, such as those at Enron and WorldCom, one of the driving factors that justified the actions of so many managers was the mistaken reliance on the opinions of various experts. Managers at Enron, for example, justified their actions by inappropriately broadening the scope of narrowly written opinions from their auditors and outside legal counsel. In hindsight, these misreadings seem negligent and even willfully obtuse. But in the heat of the battle for very profitable deals—or for survival—these opinions could be taken as islands of certainty amid the stormy seas of financial and ethical pressure.

While much has been written on the financial scandals of the early twenty-first century, a deeper look at what some of the lesser-known perpetrators were thinking offers critical insight into how organizational culture influenced key decisions. At WorldCom, for example, CEO Bernard Ebbers and CFO Scott Sullivan knowingly engaged in fraud, but it was the accounting and finance managers, such as controller David Myers, who actually made the false accounting entries. Understanding what went through their minds will be helpful in learning how to create a culture that not only prevents fraud but removes other roadblocks to performance.

In May 2008, Myers spoke to a group of ethics and compliance officers in one of his first public appearances after being released from prison. He mentioned that one of his positions before joining World-Com was in-house auditor at an insurance company in Jackson, Mississippi, that was in the process of being acquired. Leadership asked Myers not to tell employees that jobs were being moved as part of the acquisition. Later, this deception would come back to haunt him.

Sullivan, a college friend, brought Myers to WorldCom, where he was treasurer and then controller. As controller, Myers uncovered a mess. The accounting department was highly disorganized, and because of multiple acquisitions, there was never time to put all of the pieces in order. Everyone was always scrambling. WorldCom's 1997 acquisition of MCI Communications, in particular, was huge. World-Com was betting the bank that the dot-com era was just beginning, and it bought MCI in hopes of taking a leading role in building the backbone of the Internet. But the MCI and WorldCom cultures were very different, and integrating their staffs and policies was difficult. And then the recession of 2000 slammed the technology industry.

WorldCom came under increasing pressure to meet or exceed the analysts' quarterly earnings expectations. When Myers presented his numbers to Sullivan during one tense session, in which there was tremendous pressure to ensure that quarterly earnings met the analysts' forecasts, Sullivan told him, "This is garbage," insisting that the numbers were "wrong." As Myers admitted to the audience at the ethics conference, he was a "pleaser." He knew his numbers were correct and he quickly knew what was being asked of him and his colleagues to help the company get through the quarter.

Myers said that if he had been personally threatened with dismissal for not complying, he might not have done what he did. But Sullivan pushed a different set of buttons: he told Myers that WorldCom was in a desperate situation, and if Myers and his team did not make these false entries, thousands of their colleagues in Jackson, Mississippi, would lose their jobs. Did Myers really want to cause so much pain for his friends?

Myers was at a crossroads. All of us face situations where we have a struggle in our heads as to whether the right thing to do is to act for the common good or to protect ourselves. The powerful pull toward acting in our narrowest self-interest can be thwarted only if we have safeguards to clear our thinking—an aligned organizational culture that makes it easy for rationalization to be called out and for clearer thinking to prevail.

Myers let himself believe that the problem would fix itself in the next quarter. It did not, and the numbers became increasingly worse. Yet no one was willing to say anything. Everyone rationalized what he or she needed to do. Myer's staff was scared of the consequences of their actions, and many of them thought of leaving, but they just kept hoping the problem would somehow just go away. Ebbers then spoke to Controller Myers, apologizing for the position that Myers and his staff were put in."[14]

In retrospect, Myers asked himself why he did not go to Ebbers earlier and why he agreed to engage in the false accounting entries quarter after quarter. Sullivan, he said, always assured him it was a short-term issue: "Let's just get through it." As Myers put it, "We believe our own lies."

When did Myers's actions become illegal? Myers said he never really knew, which in and of itself is a statement about the WorldCom culture. The line between aggressive accounting and criminal activity was never clear to Myers or anybody else in the department. It was a case of one incremental judgment call after another. Sullivan was seen as a financial genius, and everyone wanted to believe that he had come up with a clever plan to navigate the company through its crisis. Myers did not know when he crossed the line, but once he knew that he had crossed it, he saw no way to do anything about it. The team knew that they had already screwed up. Their leaders said to them, "We will take the fall for you." Myers had no one to talk to. Bernie Ebbers had taken the position that "ethics and compliance was a waste of time" and that "all that matters is the stock price." This created the culture and the social norms at WorldCom.

Remember that Myers was only one of many managers and advisors at WorldCom who reviewed the false accounting statements before they were filed with the government. What were they all thinking? Were they complicit in the crime, or were some of them so narrowly focused on their own work they allowed themselves not to see the bigger picture? As a leader, you need to be aware of your and your people's tendency to rationalize their actions, and you need to be able to take action as early as possible to protect both them and your organization. Sometimes you need to intervene by speaking to a person you realize is facing a pressure-filled situation that could lead to rationalization. (This would be an opportunity to practice the power virtue of transparency discussed in detail in Chapter Six.) Other times you may be able to anticipate that certain policies and practices (such as any injunction to "just get it done" or "just make the numbers") are likely to put certain employees in a pressure situation that could lead to rationalization and then help those employees avoid the trap. (This would be an opportunity to practice the power virtue of integrity, discussed in detail in Chapter Four.)

Even something that is considered a best practice, such as managing by objectives, can turn out to be an occasion for rationalization. When individuals or groups have their own targets or goals, these goals may run counter to what is in the best interest of the organization. Many times the specific objectives are left vague; managers and employees are simply told to "make your numbers" or "do your best." In such an environment, the subconscious rationalization process can convince us that the ends justify the means. In many instances, the consequences may seem rather benign, but may very well be the start of the slippery slope toward greater rationalization. In a manufacturing company, for example, leadership may create performance incentives for a manager that require a certain production output. Operators and supervisors on the factory floor may complain that quality will suffer in the quest for quantity. There may not be time to fix and maintain equipment, or pressure may be applied to deliver questionable parts in order to make the numbers. But the manager may come to believe that these risks are legitimate because there is no other way to meet the production goal he has been given.

The best way to mitigate this normal human tendency is to remove the grounds for rationalization rather than try to stop people from rationalizing. As I show in Chapter Four, developing integrity, one of the power values, through consistent and predictable business practices bolsters the social norms that may discredit the viability of rationalization. This approach will help you create a culture that reduces the risks of fraud as well as improves the opportunities to operate at your highest potential.

Disengagement

In my work with organizations, one of the most difficult behavior roadblocks to overcome is a sense of apathy or not caring exemplified by, "It's not my problem," or, "Why should I get involved in this issue?" Disengaged employees can go unnoticed for a long time if they are not engaging in outright misconduct or overtly destructive behavior. But they are not taking ownership of problems and situations; rather, they are leaving critical issues unresolved because they no longer care enough to make the effort to solve them. One of the prime drivers of this sense of disengagement is the feeling that one lacks autonomy. Do we feel that we are making our own choices—or at least influencing important decisions—or do we see that we are just cogs in the machine?

I have worked for a number of years with a group of midlevel managers and engineering professionals at a U.S.-based division of a global manufacturing and aerospace company that I will call Northern Defense. In 2010, Northern Defense was coping with the changes in the defense industry as the Iraq and Afghanistan wars were winding down. The company, which had been well suited to implementing programs efficiently and effectively for many years, now faced uncertain growth as several of its established programs were scheduled to be shut down. It had to venture into new territory and identify new opportunities and even new markets. Leadership wanted to be certain that in this transition to new demands, there was nothing systemic in the culture that would hold the company back.

Northern Defense employees were well educated and well compensated, and the company expected them to be at the forefront of effective cost control while generating cutting-edge products and services. In fact, they were frustrated and demotivated. Although their job performance ratings had not yet dropped so as to warrant inquiry from their leadership, they were no longer making the extra effort their company needed to stay competitive.

One of those managers told me, "Success and failure feel the same here." The culture was not encouraging feedback or valuing inclusion.

These managers were often part of larger teams working on the specifications and financial implications of complex weapons systems. One manager told me she sometimes works weeks on an analysis of one key aspect of a project and then receives no feedback at all. "If I do a good job," she explained, "it would be nice to be told that once in a while. If I am not meeting my manager's needs, I wish he would let me know so I can improve. But the worst feeling is to not hear anything. A black hole. Am I just wasting my time?"

In another part of the company, a talented young engineer decided that contributing to team meetings to develop new approaches to quicker and more efficient delivery was not worth his efforts. He was tired of feeling belittled and not valued. "If I don't speak up," he explained, "no one will call me stupid."

For knowledge workers in particular, being well compensated is not enough. They need to feel that their work is valued and that they are contributing to the organization's overall effort. Otherwise they begin to feel frustrated and start to disengage.

Employees want to take on higher levels of personal responsibility and to be accountable and rewarded for their own actions. When I relay this desire to leaders, they are thrilled to hear that news. Their companies also want employees to take on greater responsibility and be more accountable. Why, then, is it so hard to make it happen? The reason is that many companies do not understand what really motivates their employees, in particular, the role of company culture. Although job security is obviously important and keeps employees coming to work every day, research shows that for employees whose jobs require creativity and the ability to analyze and solve problems, traditional forms of compensation and reward are insufficient to keep them motivated.

Psychologists and organizational development experts talk about two types of workplace motivation: extrinsic and intrinsic. Extrinsic motivations are the external and tangible ones, such as compensation and work conditions. For more administrative or repetitive tasks, these tangible rewards may be the only motivation that would encourage the employee's continued engagement. Intrinsic motivators are the intangible benefits of doing a job, that is, the feeling that the work itself is satisfying. This feeling can come from a sense of intellectual curiosity or a sense that the work has a greater purpose. Since intrinsic motivation is linked to one's feelings, it can be generated by challenges and accomplishments that feed both self-esteem and the sense of being appreciated. Research has shown that for work that requires trial-and-error thinking, with expectations of breaking from the path to discover a novel strategy, intrinsic rewards are the best motivators. Intrinsically motivated people see more creative solutions to problems. They allow their inherent curiosity and problem-solving skills to emerge and be given free rein.

With constant change in market conditions and technology, companies need these creative skills more than ever before. Yet most companies focus more on tangible compensation, putting less emphasis on intangible motivation. In many organizations, the intrinsic rewards are nice-to-haves that are not seen as essential to keep employees satisfied and motivated. The logic seems to be that if managers and individual contributors are well compensated, they should do their work without needing soft and fuzzy affirmation of how valuable they are. And to be fair, it's not easy for companies to provide the intrinsic motivations that will let the full creative genius of each employee emerge. That requires giving employees enough time and freedom to learn in depth, gather and process information, and make choices.

The company also needs to have—and to demonstrate—an appreciation for well-finished and well-integrated work, so that employees don't have to wonder, *Am I just wasting my time?* and don't find that "success and failure feel the same here." Although this may not be easy, the costs of not providing intrinsic motivation may be greater than leaders think.

Research has shown that the need for autonomy (the need to make choices and to feel like the initiator of one's own actions) fuels our desire to be self-motivated and to work to our highest potential.[15]

In many companies I have worked with, employees and managers seek ownership of some aspect of their jobs. They tell me, "Reward me if I do well, and I'm willing to face the consequences if I fall short, but let me be at least partly responsible for determining how I will do this aspect of my job."

When your people want more autonomy, it doesn't mean they want to cast off your leadership and do whatever they want. In fact, the more we can satisfy this need at work, the more we feel that we live the values that are meaningful to us and the more we can appreciate the processes and procedures—even the bureaucracy—that allow us to live those values and to make our own decisions and carry them out.

From my experience with helping employees manage themselves within their organization's culture, few things are as vital as making sure that they have a clear sense of where they can act autonomously. Once the mental switch for disengagement is switched on—the culture has convinced us there's no point in trying to give the company our best—we are focused only on ourselves. Like the young engineer at Northern Defense, we decide whether engaging and contributing is worth the emotional risk, recognizing that we open ourselves to push-back and even criticism. This switch is therefore our decision to take responsibility for our actions: I can either just do what I am told and get by with the minimum effort, or I can do what really needs to be done for the organization to succeed. Each employee can flip the switch either way, so the organization needs to be aware of the triggers that cause him or her to flip it on or off.

Most employees seek some level of personal responsibility for their actions; they would like their disengagement switch to be off. They want a chance to do their jobs as they have been trained to do them. This allows them to feel emotionally connected to their work and to feel that they would choose to work in this company or do this job because it satisfies an emotional need. As we will see, organizations that fulfill this personal desire are usually rewarded with a more dedicated and loyal workforce, happy to do what it takes to ensure that the organization's work is done as well as possible.

But this comes from a risk for organizations: for the kind of performance that demands knowledge workers be intrinsically motivated, there is no neutral ground. It's hard for knowledge workers to just clock in and clock out for long periods. If employees have jobs that require intrinsic motivation, failure to provide that motivation can have negative consequences because they will quickly become bored and frustrated. Although they may still be valuable knowledge workers, they are also now dangerous risk factors, if not for what they might do, then for what they will not—or will no longer—do in the way of sticking their necks out for the good of their company.

At one level, performance can suffer. I recently worked with an insurance company, which I will call Western Financial, an American subsidiary of a global insurance corporation. Western Financial was having a problem retaining the sales representatives who sold group disability and life insurance to major companies. The sales were complex because the pricing and limits for various policies had to be worked out with an independent insurance broker and with the company's own underwriting department. These employees had come to Western Financial for its entrepreneurial spirit. They liked being in control of their day and their own success. With their customers, they were independent dynamic professionals. But when they had to beg their underwriting department to take action on their cases, they became helpless cogs in the machine. The standard answer from underwriting was no. The only way a rep could get underwriting to take action was for the rep to have his or her manager escalate the matter to the underwriter's manager. The reps found this endless struggle just to do their job well a drain on their natural energy and drive. Their level of engagement began to drop, and people started to leave the company. In exit interviews, they said that their compensation was fine, but they hated having so little control over their own business. Western Financial paid the price in loss of experience, loss of collective knowledge, and the time and money spent recruiting and training new employees.

The situation can get even worse when a lack of autonomy drives otherwise normal people to cede their own sense of responsibility to others. If someone tells us that he or she will take responsibility for our actions, does that give us a free pass to do whatever we like? As we know from the Stanley Milgram experiments in the early 1960s, the power of obedience to a perceived authority cannot be ignored in understanding how people act under pressure.[16] In these classic experiments, repeated thousands of times, the volunteer participant was asked to deliver what he or she believed was a potentially lethal electric shock to a "student" who had answered a question incorrectly. The participant certainly knew that administering such a shock was inappropriate, unethical, and even immoral, but the persuasive authority of the test administrator was often sufficient to keep the participant doing it anyway. The disturbing lesson of these experiments is people's willingness to transfer their moral conscience to an authority figure who is (or claims to be) willing to accept the consequences. In 2008, the BBC broadcast a twenty-first-century version of Milgram's classic experiment. In one scene, a sensitive and empathetic man in the role of teacher was quite disturbed that he was seemingly inflicting severe pain on the "student." Several times, he got up and said he could not continue with the experiment. And yet all the leader had to do to get this empathetic teacher to continue inflicting pain was tell him that the experiment must continue and that he, the leader, would be responsible for what happened. It was that easy for one well-intentioned person to transfer his sense of personal responsibility to someone else. Recall that World-Com executives were able to get people like David Myers to keep doing things they knew were wrong by promising, "We will take the fall for you." Every day in companies everywhere, the power of the authority figure is strong enough that people who feel little autonomy are willing to forget who they are and what they stand for and go along with what the boss says.

SETTING THE STAGE FOR THE POWER VALUES

To understand and cope better with each of these three human behavior roadblocks—self-deception, rationalization, and disengagement—we need to understand our internal balance of self-interest weighed against the needs of others. For a company, high performance requires employees to balance what is important to them as individuals with what is important to the organization, its customers, and the stakeholders the organization serves. Each employee must be able to see his or her role in the organization and how his or her relationship with the organization is mutually beneficial. Otherwise there is a risk that the positive values we each have may be suppressed or supplanted by negative values, leading us to do things we are not proud of.

The organization needs to create strong social norms that dissuade self-deception, remove the sources of rationalization, and prevent the disengagement that keeps employees from taking responsibility for their actions. The challenge for leaders is to integrate these concepts into the organization's everyday training, communications, and business processes. As with losing weight, it's obvious what to do but hard to know how to do it and then actually do it. Business gurus and thought leaders regularly offer prescriptive advice to solve the challenges they have discovered through their research. Articles that address behavior-based risk issues often end with broad suggestions such as, "Brainstorm unintended consequences when devising goals and incentives," and, "Root out conflicts of interest." True enough, but to do that, the organization has to have a culture in which people can be called out on their risky, inefficient, or unacceptable behavior.

We have limitations as people. Dedicated employees become disengaged. Good people rationalize their misdeeds. Successful managers stray off course through self-deception. How can you manage the individual idiosyncrasies of each employee? In successful companies, leaders do just that. They are mindful that their employees are vulnerable to the roadblocks of rationalization, self-deception, and disengagement. These companies understand that culture shapes behavior and is something an organization can take control of in order to steer clear of those roadblocks.

The next step is to identify a framework for you to be able to sort and categorize the kinds of actions and behaviors needed to keep employees engaged and focused on common organizational goals.

Values Drive Culture

The elements of culture—the principles and beliefs, the mission and goals, and the standards of behavior—are just the placeholders for attributes that characterize the organization. Every organization has them, but what matters—what is good or bad, high performance or dysfunctional, evolving or stuck, aligned or misaligned—are the actual values (and the behaviors that go with them) of the organization as a whole and of its individual employees that fill each of these elemental buckets. Your job as a leader is to determine what values are there now, what values you need in order to have a high-performing organization, and how to make those changes happen. In this chapter, we're going to look at a useful way to classify the variety of values that exist. Then we will apply that classification to the values that are often found (or are found lacking) in companies and what that means for you and your people.

When a leader is praised for successfully turning around a culture, the focus is often on his or her will and personality. But many times what the successful leader has done is create a framework that allows the organization to right itself. He or she has identified which types of values and behaviors are important for each of the elements of culture, which of those need to be eliminated, and which values and behaviors need to be strengthened or added in order for the three elements to work together. A culture success story worth learning from is the transformation undertaken over the past few years at the Boeing Company.

Boeing, a Fortune 50 company with over 150,000 employees, had maintained a sterling reputation for two generations as an engineer-centric builder of airplanes. Employees loved the company and felt tremendous loyalty and commitment. But things changed in the late 1990s as Boeing grappled with four major scandals over a ten-year period. Each could have been seen as an isolated case, but the success of the leader who finally righted the ship was to see that each was a by-product of culture-driven shortcomings. What went wrong was at least partly a result of "how we do things around here."

The first scandal started with classic rationalization. Working under the gun to pull together a bid, a program manager at Boeing might often think how much easier his job would be if he had access to his competitors' proposals. This wish came true in 1996 when an engineer left Lockheed Martin to join Boeing and brought with him approximately twenty-five thousand pages of documents, many of which had proprietary markings from Lockheed Martin and other contractors. About a dozen people, including the "lucky" program manager, had access to the competitive information for two and a half years before anybody said anything. This ethics breach cost Boeing $1 billion in lost government business. Above and beyond the legal questions, the sheer volume of the documents astounded the prosecutors. Boeing's own general counsel, Douglas G. Bain, later demanded of his audience at the company's annual executive retreat, "How could you have that many documents floating around and nobody said anything? Why were there two-and-a-half years of silence?"[1]

The second scandal was a case of self-deception. In 2003, chief financial officer Michael Sears was actively seeking the CEO seat soon to be vacated by Phil Condit. His approach was to take advantage of Condit's weakness with the board by taking control of as many resources as he could. Sears took over all public relations responsibilities and controlled access to the media and investors, an unusual role for a CFO. "It was clear to everybody [that] Sears was anxious to be the successor to Phil to the point that it got pretty disgusting," said a Boeing board member. "You got tired of him acting like the heir apparent." In fact, such backstabbing was widespread among the top brass. "It was everybody in the suite gunning for Phil's job," said a former senior Boeing executive. "It was pretty destructive."[2]

In Sears's mind, the final step to secure the CEO position was to do something his competitors for the position had not been able to do: recruit influential U.S. Air Force procurement officer Darleen Druyun to a senior position at Boeing. Druyun was looking to move to the private sector, and with her contacts and her understanding of the Pentagon procurement process, she was possibly the most sought-after executive-to-be in the defense industry. Boeing and most of its rivals tried hard to land her, but federal regulations severely limited the ability of federal employees to actively seek positions in the private sector. Sears was able to seal the deal with her, giving him an advantage over his rivals and the potential to expand his power base by making Druyun an ally. The only problem was that Sears and Druyun had to break the law to close the deal, and both served time in prison for their illegal job negotiations. Sears might have had criminal intent all along, but it is more likely that in a company culture in which cutthroat competition was the norm, he was able to convince himself that what he was doing was a necessary way to beat out his competitors.

An unhealthy focus on internal politics wasn't Boeing's only culture problem. In March 2004, Boeing agreed to pay $70 million to settle a class action suit alleging widespread sexual discrimination. Sexual misconduct by executives was also a problem and a frequent topic of conversation among employees. CEO Phil Condit settled at least one wrongful-termination lawsuit brought by a female employee with whom he had had a relationship.

After the documents scandal, the Druyun scandal, the sexual discrimination settlement, and Condit's sexual harassment troubles, Boeing's board felt the company needed an exemplary leader—a Boy

Scout—in the top spot. This in itself was an example of the typical emphasis on the leader's own qualities. As we will see, it was the qualities of the organization itself rather than the qualities of any particular leader that were the heart of the matter.

The board asked Harry Stonecipher, the former head of McDonnell Douglas, to come out of retirement and calm the waters. One of Stonecipher's top goals as Boeing's new CEO was to put ethics front and center. He created an internal governance office, reporting to him, and required every employee to sign an ethics statement. He set a standard of zero tolerance for any breach of the newly revised code of ethics. "Without integrity you cannot conduct business successfully," he wrote in the June 2004 issue of Boeing's in-house magazine. "Firing people who lack integrity is good business."[3] Within two years, however, details emerged about Stonecipher's personal relationship with a female Boeing executive. Even though she did not report directly to him, Stonecipher resigned.

How can an organization know where to start to get its culture back on track? Most organizations fall back on the antiquated notion that if employees only knew better, they wouldn't get themselves and the company into trouble. It's the corporate equivalent of having the errant schoolchild write, "I promise not to cheat on my tests," a hundred times on the blackboard. After the scandals, Boeing did what organizations with similar problems often do: it commissioned a blue-ribbon panel that recommended a back-to-basics approach of increasing mandatory ethics and compliance training. But Boeing's 150,000 employees did not need to be reminded what the rules were. They knew the right thing to do. Those who broke rules knew they were doing so, but they had other reasons for thinking that's what they had to do. What they needed was a clear road map showing how they could do the right thing even when it seemed that they needed to do the wrong thing—that is, a guide to navigating the pitfalls presented by the company culture and their own human nature.

To address its troubles, Boeing needed to go beyond looking just at behavior and get to the root causes of its scandals. It needed to know why clearly unacceptable behavior was allowed to persist throughout the organization. It needed to answer general counsel Bain's question: How could this have been going on when so many people knew? Although the analytical engineers at Boeing may not have liked to hear it, what their company needed was to understand the psychological motivations of its 150,000 employees.

Jim McNerney, a former head of 3M who succeeded the disgraced Harry Stonecipher as CEO of Boeing in 2005, understood that Boeing's problem was not the rules but the culture—"how we do things around here." The path that McNerney laid out for Boeing illustrates a framework that I have used successfully in helping organizations categorize the myriad behaviors needed to create a positive culture: he made an effort to identify the values and behaviors that made up Boeing's principles and beliefs, its mission and goals, and its standards of behavior. Then he began to take steps to eliminate the negative values that were preventing those positive values embodied by employees to be lived in the company day to day.

LEVELS OF AWARENESS

I don't know if famed psychologist Abraham Maslow was on Jim McNerney's mind as he started his work at Boeing, but he should have been. Maslow looked at the factors that motivate positive and negative behaviors.[4] For example, why are some people more susceptible to acting on the inclinations we all have? We all have thoughts about rationalizing misdeeds. We all are vulnerable to self-deception. We all are susceptible to becoming disengaged when we are frustrated by a lack of autonomy. What causes some people to go over the edge, while others control these emotions and move on? We all are susceptible to the three deep-seated anxieties or fears that are at the heart of Maslow's work: fear of failure, fear of being unliked, and fear of being left out. Because of these fears—and perhaps through our subconscious—we can be incredibly focused (sometimes obsessed) on unfulfilled needs for power, fame, or acceptance. Managers who act contrary to their values, or at least to the social norms of their organizations, do so in large part because of these unfulfilled needs.

We can hope that at some point, we overcome our fears and achieve enough self-awareness to see what motivates our behavior and how we relate to others. Most of us can achieve self-fulfillment when we see how we are connected to others and the world around us. As we will see, despite the surface-level focus on individual achievement that permeates our business environment, the vast majority of employees seek a sense of connection to others and to the larger goals of their organizations. For organizational leaders, then, the goal should be to help each employee become the best he or she can be by acknowledging and overcoming his or her fears. I am not suggesting that the key to high performance is providing each employee with a private therapist to help deal with unmet needs. The legacy of work by Lewin and others in understanding the role of the environment in shaping behavior will make our job much easier. We can focus on the barriers that cause people and organizations to detour into trouble and the means with which to reduce the impact of these barriers.

Richard Barrett, an author and social commentator on the evolution of human values in business and society, developed a model that builds on Maslow's hierarchy of needs to create the linkage between our motivations—our underlying fears and needs—and behavior.[5] Understanding these largely unconscious motivators and barriers, and then framing that understanding in the language of business, can guide organizations in motivating the employee behaviors they need for high performance without needless risk.

The range of our fears and motivators, as well as our capacity for self-actualization, can be categorized as *levels of awareness,* a classification of one's concern with either a particular type of danger or threat or else a particular type of aspiration. Within each level of awareness is a variety of related beliefs and behaviors that we call values. This is a particularly useful categorization for leaders because it highlights the depths of the fears that must be addressed, as well as how far a workforce can be stretched toward achieving higher goals. You need to see which fears are the deepest and therefore need to be addressed first so that they don't undermine everything else you try to do.

We can operate at multiple levels of awareness simultaneously, but our primary level of awareness will have the most influence on how we see ourselves and the world, including the world of work in which most of us spend so many of our waking hours. What if you knew how your employees perceived their lives inside the organization? What if you could determine which level of awareness would most empower your employees to help the organization meet its business goals? What if each of your employees could assess his or her own deficiencies as well as his or her level of self-actualization in a way that lent itself to a collective understanding of your organizational culture? You could then see that your employees are challenged by fears, frustrations, and roadblocks, and you could see what you need to do to help them overcome these obstacles to their self-actualization, which are also your organization's obstacles to high performance.

Understanding your workforce's levels of self-awareness and consciousness is vital, but these concepts have been seen as far too intangible for pragmatic business leaders to grasp. Yet, perhaps intuitively, leaders such as Jim McNerney, who create (or restore) high-performing organizational cultures, address these categories of self-deficiency and self-awareness head-on.

McNerney spent his first six months at the helm learning about Boeing's culture, including the many subcultures that make up such a large organization. McNerney saw how the employees from acquired companies had a different view of the business than legacy Boeing employees did. McDonnell Douglas, for example, had a culture of intense internal competition, very different from the collegial culture of Boeing, which had merged with McDonnell Douglas in 1997. McNerney also saw how employees in different functions and projects saw their work and the company differently. In an interview after this initial tour of the company, McNerney said that the overall Boeing culture had become "dysfunctional" in some places. In particular, there was a culture of silence rooted in internal balkanization and rivalries. He concluded that "too many people who thought something 'didn't feel right' failed to raise a red flag for a variety of reasons. They wanted to win a contract, they feared retaliation, they just didn't want to rock the boat, or they lacked the courage to speak up in a command-and-control culture. I feel that you have to create a work environment that encourages people to talk about the tough issues—business- or ethics-related—and to make the right decisions when they find themselves at the crossroads between hitting their numbers for the quarter and stepping forward when there's a problem."[6]

In the terms of this book, McNerney was describing an organization where principles, goals, and standards were not aligned. There's nothing dysfunctional about expecting managers to hit their numbers or about top executives competing to be the next CEO; what was dysfunctional was the lack of checks and balances that tempered these normal but aggressive drives. Boeing's culture had weakened the counterweights of the collective good against self-interest. People who should have known better did not speak up when they saw something wrong.

Boeing's culture was not only getting it into legal trouble; it was also diminishing its performance and competitiveness. McNerney found that internal rivalries were not only at the root of the company's ethical scandals but were also preventing managers from cutting costs and sharing good ideas. For example, Boeing was buying two hundred different kinds of safety glasses and eighty varieties of white paper. "Why can't we buy two or three different kinds of safety glasses?" asked James F. Albaugh, CEO of Boeing Integrated Defense Systems. "It's all about making us one company. It will give us leverage and make us dependent on each other for success."[7]

McNerney explicitly connected Boeing's values with its performance: "If we can get the values lined up with performance, then this is an absolutely unbeatable company."[8] As you will see in the discussion of levels of awareness, McNerney took steps to address Boeing's culture at the various levels of awareness at which he found problems.

THE SEVEN LEVELS OF AWARENESS

There are leaders such as Jim McNerney who have an intuitive sense of how to identify the root causes of their organization's cultural problems. A more systematic approach for the rest of us is to use a model that helps leaders bridge the inner world of Maslow's needs with the pragmatic requirements of creating an effective corporate culture. Richard Barrett's model helps companies make the intuitive work of leaders such as McNerney tangible and actionable. In my work I call Barrett's model the Seven Levels of Awareness.[9]

Each level embodies basic human fears and aspirations. As we become aware of them, we can shape the experiences around us that would otherwise lead us to do the bad things we want to stop and that could instead encourage us to reach the higher goals we dream of. Each level of awareness also embodies distinct values, which guide our behavior. Table 3.1 shows the seven levels with examples of individual and organizational values and behaviors at each level.

Table 3.1   Seven Levels of Awareness

Level of Awareness		Examples of Values at Each Level	
		Individual	**Organizational**
1	Survival	Health, Caution, Control	Profit, Short-term focus
2	Relationship	Family, Respect, Caring	Open communication, Employee recognition, Blame
3	Performance	Being organized, Achievement	Best practices, Bureaucracy, Inconsistency
4	Engagement	Adaptability, Responsibility	Accountability, Innovation, Teamwork
5	Communal	Cooperation, Trust	Commitment, Integrity, Transparency
6	Contribution	Making a difference, Mentoring	Collaboration, Employee fulfillment
7	Service	Compassion, Humility	Long-term perspective, Vision

Levels 1 to 3

The first three levels of awareness focus on the basics. As individuals, we address the vital areas of survival, relationships, and self-esteem at these levels. For organizations, these levels address how well they balance the need to stay in business, whether employees have productive or destructive personal relationships at work, and whether the organization can get its work done effectively and competitively. By addressing the awareness challenges, you help your people balance the external influences on their personal decision making that can lead to self-deception, rationalization, and disengagement.

Since these three lower levels are aligned with basic human fears, there are both positive and limiting values, which result in constructive and dysfunctional behaviors, respectively. Although it is unlikely that any company leaders would say they want the company to have values such as "bureaucracy," "blame," and "confusion," they allow these traits to persist and flourish to the extent that employees experience them as being a major feature of "how we do things around here." That makes them values as I am defining the term. And these values do, after all, address some basic fears and needs, although not as productively and satisfyingly as more positive and aligned values could do.

Level 1: Survival Awareness

Survival is essential, but we are dangerously limited if that is all we can think about. People need to feel confident about their survival before they can address more advanced needs. As employees, people need to feel confident about the organization's survival—which is to say, their ability to earn a living—before they can address more advanced organizational needs. Individual values at this level include positive values such as caution, health, job security, and wealth, as well as potentially limiting values such as control. Organizational values at this level include positive values such as cost reduction, employee health, and profit, as well as negative values such as exploitation, risk aversion, and short-term focus.

Organizations must have a healthy focus on the bottom line, but without allowing this focus to block out other values that will sustain longer-term success. Many leaders say to me that profit should be the only value they need at their company, and nothing else should matter. I say back to them, "How do you tell your employees to make a profit?" If the answer is limited to level 1, the response can be as blunt as, "Just do it." There is no other vocabulary. The leaders cannot articulate ways to make a profit based on higher levels of awareness. But an exclusive focus on meeting the quarterly numbers can lead to excessive control, micromanagement, and risk aversion. It is in such companies that the excessive obedience to authority that Milgram identified may be most prevalent, as we saw with David Myers's suppression of his own better nature in obedience to his bottom-line-obsessed bosses at WorldCom.

Employees in some organizations work under a constant cloud of fear. If they do not fear losing their own jobs, they fear that their division will be sold off. Most employees today understand the general uncertainty of the market and the dynamic of continual change; they don't expect an impossible level of security. But they are often not getting much help from leadership in managing their legitimate fears. This is not a matter of coddling oversensitive employees but of nurturing rather than squandering the organization's capacity for high performance. For example, I worked with an aircraft manufacturer where I found the employees increasingly paralyzed by fear, a reasonable response as they saw key contracts not being renewed and heard constant rumors of imminent layoffs. The predictable result was that they were becoming increasingly self-centered, with an unsustainable focus on the immediate bottom line to the exclusion of the longer-term health of the company. Adding to the danger was the fact that employees who will do anything to keep their company alive for another few months are at great risk of doing something that will damage or destroy it; David Myers was just such a one.

In other organizations, fear is less overt, but there is a deep-seated sense that making the numbers is all that matters. In such companies, brass-tacks values such as control, job insecurity, short-term focus, excessive focus on the bottom line, and pressure to make the numbers often crowd out the ability to focus on innovation, quality, or partnering with customers—values that are rooted in higher levels of awareness.

For many managers and many organizational cultures, a survival-of-the-fittest attitude creates a zero-sum culture in which winning is truly the only thing that matters, regardless of the collateral damage. Boeing as a whole was never in danger of going out of business, even during the worst of its scandals, but Jim McNerney found pockets within the firm where a win-at-any-cost attitude shaped how employees and managers juggled their goals and standards of behavior. "Win at any cost" is easy to understand and can provide an immediate reward. Your challenge as a leader in an organization where managers take that approach is to help people assess not just the benefits but also the costs of winning. For Boeing, winning at any cost poisoned the key relationships, particularly with the U.S. government, that are essential in the big-ticket defense and aerospace industry. Long-term trust can be quantifiably more valuable than a short-term win. Michael Sears's win-at-any-cost approach certainly cost him, Darleen Druyun, and Boeing far more than was gained.

Level 2: Relationship Awareness
We are social animals, and having relationships is vital to our individual mental health and stability. It is also the cornerstone of almost any kind of work within an organization. Every organization needs harmonious interpersonal relationships and good internal communications to ensure that day-to-day work is done efficiently and effectively, without controversy and distraction. Individual values at this level include positive values such as caring, friendship, and respect, as well as limiting values such as being liked (which may reflect a poor self-image). Organizational values at this level include positive values such as listening, respect, and employee appreciation, as well as limiting values such as blame, manipulation, and empire building. Organizations can help their people work effectively at this level by ensuring that the organization supports values, such as open communication

and employee recognition, that reflect caring, belonging, loyalty, and mutual responsibility.

We cannot forget how vulnerable we are with regard to relationships or to our fears of being unliked or left out. Employees don't need to feel loved, but they need to feel respected and to know that their supervisors are watching out for them and that they can speak up without fear.[10] It's good to keep in mind the lessons of the Asch conformity studies, discussed in Chapter Two, on how easy it is to rationalize misconduct in order to save face with the group or gain its approval. Because of our human desire to feel included, employees always suspect the worst when leaders meet behind closed doors or fail to communicate effectively. This is also the case when blame, secrecy, internal competition, empire building, information hoarding, and a silo mentality indicate that leaders are more focused on their own personal success than on the success of the organization. When interpersonal relationships are poor, the tendency is for people to go against their better judgment in order to feel included. An organization needs to be mindful of situations in which its employees would rather conform—to avoid upsetting social norms—than do the right thing. At best, the time and emotional energy spent in navigating relationship-level hazards is a distraction from the organization's most critical work. At worse, it poses a serious risk.

Jim McNerney saw the need to focus on the relationship level of awareness when he sought to open up Boeing's culture. Internal rivalries stemming from previous mergers were still driving wedges between teams and groups that needed to work together. People were not speaking up. For previous Boeing leaders, this had not been a priority. Tough engineers, they thought, did not need to be pampered by dealing with soft issues such as respect and an open-door policy. McNerney took a different approach, trying to lead by example. He won early praise from coworkers for paying attention to the small things: remembering people's names, listening closely to their presentations, and not embarrassing anyone in public. Why would such small things matter? This is a sincere question I often hear from executives. As we will see, when employees perceive that they are not respected, this belief has a major impact on how engaged they are—including whether they would report misconduct.

Fortunately, employees are less likely today than in the past to encounter outright physical humiliation or exploitation on the job. Your challenges as a leader are more subtle now. At Northern Defense, for example, employees were frustrated by the inconsistent application of rules and policies due to management by intimidation. Some managers and directors there used abusive behavior to maintain influence and control (empire building) and—as they saw it—to get the work done. These managers favored certain employees over others, so people were never sure what policies were really in force and for whom. A pervasive perception was that if you went against such managers, you would be subject to retaliation.

Level 3: Performance Awareness

We need to feel good about ourselves. Self-esteem is healthy for us as individuals and for the organization. Employees who feel confident at the performance level of awareness are not fearful and are less likely to engage in negative behaviors. Individual values at this level include positive values such as achievement, pride, responsibility, and being organized, as well as potentially limiting values such as being overly competitive. Organizational values at this level include positive values such as best practices, consistency, and professionalism, as well as limiting values such as bureaucracy, firefighting, inconsistency, and confusion. When I talk to a group of high-performing employees who are frustrated, I usually find that 60 to 70 percent of the negative values they identify in their company are at the performance level of awareness—values that keep them from doing as good a job as they want to do. At this level of awareness, then, you need to make sure not to create an environment in which risky short-term actions can be rationalized as "the only way to get things done around here." The sales professionals of a software company I worked with were so frustrated by what they considered the heavy-handed restrictions of the legal department that they would openly tell their customers and prospects, "Don't worry. We can find a way to get around legal." In their own eyes, they were trying to satisfy their customers and help their company succeed despite itself, but their approach was clearly a disaster waiting to happen.

To support employees at this level of awareness, the organization focuses on becoming the best it can be, emphasizing performance, results, and quality and taking care to use effective and consistent systems, processes, and best practices. Notice that a focus on performance does not have to mean winning at all costs. The challenge is to ensure that your organization, in its quest for high performance, does not create structures that are so hierarchical and rigid that they thwart individual achievement and responsibility. In particular, bureaucracy, a silo mentality, and inconsistent policies and procedures (even inconsistent information storage systems) are more dangerous than organizations often take them to be. Precisely because they most intensely frustrate those employees who most intensely want to get the job done, they invite workarounds that can get their company in all kinds of trouble.

Jim McNerney saw that Boeing's siloized business practices were not only perpetuating inefficiency (for example, through enormously wasteful and inefficient purchasing by individual units), but were also exacerbating the growing frustrations that were impeding good decision making. He understood that changing key systems and processes would change behavior. For example, he used compensation to influence behavior by changing what was rewarded: he linked a manager's compensation to his or her collaboration with other units, adherence to ethics rules, promotion of integrity, and avoidance of abusive behavior.

Levels 4 to 7

Reducing the limiting values at levels 1, 2, and 3 helps prevent bad things from happening and removes some of the major roadblocks to performance. But to truly achieve a high-performing culture, you need to put the positive values at the higher levels to work. The positive values at levels 4 and 5, for example, allow employees to participate fully in the organization and invite them to put the organization's interests before self-interest. Levels 6 and 7 reflect values that demonstrate awareness outside the walls of the organization. Level 6 values reflect deeper relationships to people, through collaborating and partnering. At level 7, employees are aware of their roles in a higher sense of service to country, the planet, or God.

Level 4: Engagement Awareness

At this level of awareness, people can look beyond their own self-interests and begin inquiring more broadly as to their role in the world. They can get beyond seeing themselves as helpless victims with no control over their lives. They begin the search for meaning. It is a big step for many to be able to make their own choices and begin to find a voice in the world. People who can live their lives at this level of awareness have succeeded in reducing some of the fears that hinder people at the lower levels. They can make the shift away from always watching their own backs to watching each other's backs and watching their company's back. Individual values at this level include positive values such as accountability, initiative, and resilience. Organizational values at this level include positive values such as accountability, information sharing, teamwork, and even providing employees with an opportunity for work-life balance.

Organizations can support this level of awareness by creating opportunities for employees to learn, adapt, and innovate and by nurturing empowerment, participation, and teamwork. People learn to engage by becoming aware that they have something valuable to offer. The benefit to the organization is that employees are willing to risk expressing their opinions and take responsibility for their actions. This becomes a critical gateway to greater accountability, itself a cornerstone of organizational health and high performance.

In order for organizations to thrive at this level of awareness, leaders must seek and support employees' ideas and opinions. Everyone must feel that he or she has a voice and that it will be heard. This exchange of views may require managers and leaders to admit that they do not have all the answers themselves and to invite participation. One of the challenges at this level of awareness is to avoid becoming overly biased toward consensus. Most employees do not seek the authority to make decisions; they merely seek to be heard.

Soon after Jim McNerney took charge at Boeing, he told a global forum of company leaders that too many executives had become used to "hiding in the bureaucracy." In terms of level 4 awareness, they had become too self-focused and were not making decisions for the good of Boeing. In large organizations, it can be very easy for managers to avoid making decisions—to "kick the can down the road"—almost indefinitely. There is always one more piece of information to check or opinion to seek, and decisions can be delayed until they are no longer relevant. At Boeing, hiding behind bureaucracy and processes to avoid making tough decisions was not just an ethics risk; it was a productivity and innovation risk, inimical to the health of the aerospace company.

For many companies I work with, the goal of the leader is to help his or her staff feel safe and empowered to work at this engagement level of awareness. Organizations that have succeeded in using the power values to align their culture see employees use words such as *teamwork, accountability, innovation,* and *responsibility* to describe their current work culture.

Level 5: Communal Awareness

Most of us have a need to feel that we are part of a work community that shares our values. People who operate at the communal level of awareness want to feel connected and to feel that they are a key part of a larger whole. Once people have a good sense of who they are, they can seek out kindred spirits who share their values. Most people like to be around others who are comfortable with who they are and whose values are easy to see and understand. Making this possible gives your people the courage to live their own values, a huge advantage to your organization in terms of performance and ethics. By the same token, not being able to fulfill that need is a source of frustration and therefore of risk to your organization in terms of both performance and ethics.

Individual values at this level include positive values such as cooperation, fairness, generosity, and patience. Organizational values include positive values such as creativity, loyalty, passion, and shared vision. In particular, they include the 3 power values of commitment, integrity, and transparency that make it possible for your people to live their own core values and the organization's core values at work. Communal awareness is the heart of the power values.

In my experience working with global organizations, employees embody more personal values at the communal level of awareness than at any of the other levels. The values at this level are also those that the organization needs for top performance. Level 5, then, is the sweet spot where both individual and collective needs are best met. Communal values are what Johnson & Johnson had going for it in the heyday of the Credo and what Boeing had going for it in its heyday as the dream company for people who loved building airplanes. Both companies subsequently developed cultures that violated their own communal values—cultures of expedience, secrecy, or rivalry. Jim McNerney managed to restore Boeing by focusing on its communal level of awareness, but it doesn't seem as if any leader has done the same yet at Johnson & Johnson.

The critical challenge for organizations operating at this level of awareness is developing a shared vision for the future and a shared set of values. A shared vision clarifies the organization's intentions and gives employees a unifying purpose and direction. Shared values provide guidance on decision making and create consistency in action throughout the organization. Translating the organization's values into specific behaviors and competencies provides parameters that define the boundaries of acceptable practice. The organization's values and behaviors are then reflected in all its processes and systems, with appropriate consequences for anyone not willing to walk the talk.

A critical precondition for success at this level of awareness is to build a climate of trust. Employees must feel that their values are in alignment with the organization's values (creating a sense of commitment), that the organization's actions are consistent and predictable, and that employees are free to raise issues and ask questions when they see variations from those norms. Jim McNerney began to encourage managers to talk more openly about Boeing's severe ethical lapses. "I want to try to make it okay to have that dialogue," he said. The scandals at Boeing aren't "something that happened in a separate part of the company that half of us aren't responsible for."[11] As I will show, the values that demonstrate this level of awareness are powerful in helping organizations remove the roadblocks to performance, such as self-deception, rationalization, and disengagement.

Coincidentally—or perhaps not—Jim Collins's definition of the ideal leader at his own level 5 includes many of the attributes of alignment awareness at Barrett's level 5: "Level 5 leaders channel their ego needs away from themselves and into the larger goal of building a great company. It's not that Level 5 leaders have no ego or self-interest. Indeed, they are incredibly ambitious—but their ambition is first and foremost for the institution, not themselves."[12]

Level 6: Contribution Awareness

At this level of awareness, people see the importance of their role in helping others. They have a sense of how they can make a difference in the world and are able to take steps to fulfill that mission. Since no one can change the world alone, people operating at this level seek out others with whom they can collaborate on their missions. Individual values at this level include positive values such as community service, mentoring, and personal fulfillment. Organizational values include positive values such as collaboration, customer partnerships, leadership development, and making a difference.

When I work with managers to help them develop a shared vision for their organization, I ask about their core motivations: "Beyond the paycheck, why do you come to work every day?" For many managers, the core motivation is the desire to make a positive difference in the lives of their coworkers or customers. People operating at this level of awareness therefore seek deep relationships with those around them. Timberland, the focus of Chapter Six, is an impressive example of a company operating at this level of awareness.

Organizations seeking to operate at this level of awareness see the importance of having more collaborative partnerships with a wider range of external stakeholder groups. For example, instead of fighting public interest groups, more and more companies are looking for ways to find common ground and work with them. These organizations are creating strategic alliances and partnerships with other organizations, such as suppliers or even competitors, as well as with broader stakeholder groups, such as the community. The focus at this level of awareness is deepening the interconnectedness within the organization as well as expanding its external connections. Internally, employees are collaborating with one another in developing much deeper partnerships and working relationships. Externally, the organization is a partner with other individuals and organizations that are intent on making a difference in the world through policies or practices.

Level 7: Service Awareness

At this level of awareness, we find those rare people whose determination to make a difference in the world drives them to act with the deepest sense of selfless service to others and to God, country, or the earth. These are the leaders who operate with the most profound humility and compassion. Individual values at this level include positive ones such as compassion, humility, and wisdom. Organizational values at this level include positive values such as a long-term perspective, philanthropy, and vision.

Leaders who seek to operate at this level of awareness focus on social responsibility and doing the right thing for its own sake. They understand their responsibility as stewards of the long-term success of both their own organizations and their external stakeholders. The critical issue at this level of awareness is developing a deep sense of social and environmental responsibility throughout the organization by embedding those values into all of the organization's actions.

Many people live fulfilled lives without needing to operate at this level. The same is true for organizations. Aspiring to be a level 7 organization is not the goal unless the organization wants it to be. This is just as true for the other levels. There is no formula for an organization to follow to help its employees avoid feeling the fear and pressure that lead to self-deception, rationalization, or disengagement. The key is collective self-awareness: the organization must know the capabilities of its people and the challenges they are likely to face and must equip them properly for the journey ahead.

BUILDING BLOCKS OF ALIGNMENT

Although all of us personally embody values that fall across many of the seven levels of awareness, each of us has our own strong suits that shape our character and personality. Some people are more focused on individualistic values relating to self-esteem, while others embody more relationship values or other outwardly focused values such as making a difference or caring. Similarly, every business has its own culture, reflecting myriad different values at different levels of awareness. Which levels of awareness will create a high-performing culture? The more appropriate question, since different organizations are trying to accomplish different things, is this: Which levels of awareness will create *your* high-performing culture? How can you know which combination of values to seek and encourage among your employees?

Much of the rest of the book discusses how to align the elements of your culture to create a high-performing organization. But first you need to create a picture of what that end state looks like. What kind of culture are you looking for? Although the power values of commitment, integrity, and transparency will help you to effect the desired alignment of principles, goals, and standards, you must first determine which particular values are needed in order to create the particular kind of high-performing culture you seek.

Remember that in any dynamic high-performing culture, the component values will be characterized by two kinds of alignment:

- Employees can live their personal principles and beliefs at work; that is, they see their core values reflected in the values of the work culture around them. Employees who value honesty, for example, can come to work, behave honestly, and be treated honestly. Employees usually feel this alignment when the organization has worked to ensure that its mission and goals are compatible with its employees' principles and beliefs (creating commitment), and through transparency, it protects the ability of employees to act consistently with their own principles and beliefs.

- The values that employees feel are essential for the organization to be high performing are in fact the same as those that leadership has identified as being essential to meet strategic objectives. For example, an organization will not achieve cultural alignment if leadership is pushing for an external focus on customers while employees feel that what they need in order to do their best work is better internal teamwork. As we will see in Chapter Five, this tension has an impact on both commitment and engagement.

To determine whether your culture is contributing positively to organizational performance, you need to know what your employees' principles and beliefs are now and how the behaviors resulting from them affect your organization's culture and performance. McNerney, for example, determined that many Boeing employees believed in a principle of making sure their own team beat other teams in their company and came out on top. The behaviors resulting from this principle may have included positive behaviors such as hard work and team effort, but they definitely included negative behaviors such as keeping useful information secret and undermining the efforts of others— inefficient and risky behaviors.

One tool I use to identify the employees' personal values (their principles and beliefs) and the values they see in the organization is an assessment that asks participants to choose values from a list of approximately one hundred terms, each of which corresponds to one of the seven levels of awareness.[13]

Dominance of Personal Values at the Communal Level of Awareness

I first ask participants to choose ten terms from the list of one hundred that reflect who they are as people. There are many fine attributes and characteristics to choose from—for example, caring, respect, family, being organized, and achievement. And yet in conducting such values assessments, I have been surprised by how consistent the responses have been in all types of companies all over the world. Employees choose values from all seven levels of awareness, but the level that most frequently reflects how employees see themselves is level 5: the communal level of awareness.

Whether I am working with organizations in financial services, manufacturing, or software, 28 to 30 percent of the values chosen as personal values are consistently at the communal awareness level.[14] Although values such as family, respect, reliability, and being organized are frequently in the top ten, the dominant choices have been honesty, integrity, positive attitude, and commitment. These are the values that reflect our desire to find meaning in our work and to be around those who share similar outlooks and ambitions. Employees at the communal level of awareness want to feel that they are helping the organization achieve its goals. They want to be held accountable, they want to be around others who share that sense of personal responsibility, and they are not afraid to take emotional risks by saying what is on their minds, because they value openness and honesty in their relationships. Most employees want to be able to feel that they are part of a larger group and want to have their personal success be tightly integrated with the group's success.

When I conduct focus groups and interviews with employees and managers to learn more about who they are and why they chose these particular values, I consistently find that these values are the motivators that can keep people engaged. Typically employees and managers enjoy the people with whom they work (even if that enjoyment does not extend beyond the circle of the immediate work group). They value being counted on, and they expect transparent and evenhanded interactions with others in the organization.

Fairness, another level 5 communal value, is also an important value for employees to see in the workplace. As you will see in Chapter Four, fairness is at the heart of integrity. To stay committed to the group's goals and repress the various human tendencies toward self-interest, employees must feel confident that they are being treated fairly. They are willing to be vulnerable and will trust their leaders to look out for their interests as part of the whole group as long as they do not feel that they are being taken advantage of. This sense of fairness takes in not only compensation but also opportunities for advancement and the team's opportunity to achieve its stated goals. Fairness is deeply linked to intrinsic motivation, discussed in Chapter Two. Perceptions of what is fair are subjectively influenced by how integrated and connected the individual feels to the organization. Why else would assistants, aides, and pages put up with long hours and low wages just to work with entertainers, athletes, and politicians? They don't think they are being treated unfairly, because they love what they are doing.

Organizations that make it possible for their employees to live these communal awareness values at work are the ones that enjoy a sense of internal cohesion. Their employees are looking out for ways to make sure the organization succeeds. They are watching the organization's back, anxious not to let the organization make a mistake. People tend to know what is expected of them, and there is greater consistency in decision making throughout the organization, with consequently fewer surprises. Organizations achieve this level of awareness by developing and supporting behaviors that encourage employee fulfillment. They understand that focusing on the needs of their employees will engage them, which encourages personal productivity and creativity. With a higher degree of trust, people are willing to take risks to explore new ideas and raise questions. Innovation and problem solving are more likely because there is less fear of failure when there is an opportunity to learn from mistakes.

Challenges in the Current Culture
That Thwart Alignment

When employees have high expectations of themselves and of their organization, the opportunity for achievement is greater; but there is also a greater distance to fall when the organization cannot live up to these expectations. In the values assessments I administer to employees, I present a second list of one hundred or so terms and ask them to choose ten that reflect their work environment. This list includes not only the attributes that make up the personal values list, but also some that are specific to business, including positive values such as best practices, corporate citizenship, mission focus, and strategic alliances, and limiting values such as bureaucracy, blame, firefighting, inconsistency, and confusion.

Over the years, the results of these assessments have consistently revealed two challenges organizations face. First, in most organizations, there is too little overlap between the values that are most characteristic of the organization and the values that are most important to its employees as individuals. For example, although 28 percent of employees' personal values are at the communal level of awareness, these values typically make up only about 10 percent of the organizational values that employees identify; communal values tend to be pushed aside by survival-related and performance-related values such as cost reduction, customer satisfaction, continuous improvement, profit, and productivity. While these are of course important values, overemphasizing them at the expense of the communal values that employees personally embrace generates frustration. You need to consider whether these survival- and performance-related values should be the primary focus of the culture or should be counted on as the natural outcome of a well-aligned team working together thanks to its strong communal values.

Creating a sense of alignment and shared purpose is increasingly difficult in a large organization with a matrix organizational structure in which employees report to bosses and provide value to people who are not in the same building—possibly not even in the same state or country. As employees feel less emotional connection to the people with whom they work, they start to feel that they are not adding value and become less productive and more likely to focus on their self-interest. As you will see with the disengaged employees at a corporate head-quarters in Chapter Five, this can create a distraction of time and focus at best and an invitation to undesirable behavior at worst.

Recall the talented young manager at Northern Defense who was unnerved by getting no response at all to the reports she prepared for her boss and was feeling the consequences of a lack of autonomy. She had joined the company because she believed in its mission of support-ing U.S. troops. She enjoyed her colleagues and made friends easily. Collectively, though, this group did not feel valued by the company. The sense of isolation that affected their personal autonomy also affected their sense of belonging to a larger whole. "I want to be part of a team," she explained, "not just an anonymous cog in the wheel."

This conscientious hard worker had become so frustrated that she had already begun to disengage and stop caring. She wasn't necessarily going to quit her job before finding another, but she was no longer making the extra effort that Northern Defense needed her to put forth. And at this point, who knows whether she would be willing to stick her neck out if she saw something wrong going on that should be reported? In my estimation, here was someone who by all rights should have been an ideal employee but had become an organizational risk because of her organization's culture.

Employees who operate at a high level of communal awareness need feedback. The organization cannot communicate to them too much. They want to be involved and feel secure that they are valued. Is that a bad thing? Are such employees "too needy"? When an orga-nization has people who care, leaders need to be cognizant of how to nurture this extremely valuable resource.

There is also a dangerous gap at the engagement level of awareness. Employees and managers who seek to take ownership of their actions will be frustrated by a culture or subculture in which it is easy for those who are supposed to lead to hide in the bureaucracy. The pace of work today is intense, and decisions must be made constantly to keep a project moving forward, but in a large organization, it is easy for managers to play it safe by not stepping up to make decisions that they are in fact empowered to make.

In my meetings at Lothrop Financial, for example, managers told me how frustrating it was not to be able to get answers from other parts of the organization. In order to meet aggressive sales goals, everyone needed to keep the process moving. "But," I was told, "people are scared to death to make decisions that they have authority to make."

The challenge with this kind of behavior is that it is not wrong. No rules are being violated. But nothing gets done quickly or efficiently. Employees and managers recognize that this is a far cry from high performance and want the leaders who are empowered to make decisions to make them.

Besides having too few communal values, the second challenge for most organizations is that they have too many negative values. These negative values correspond to the unfulfilled needs (to succeed, to be liked, to be included) and the related fears (failure, not being liked, being left out) that are influential at levels 1, 2, and 3. I find that most organizations have over 10 percent of their current culture values "in the red," and I have worked with companies where over 50 percent of the values were negative. This means that over half of an employee's emotional energy is focused on dealing with negative issues such as infighting and ferreting out secrets rather than on being productive. The impact is dramatic: these negative values generate the frustrations that open the door to self-deception, rationalization, and disengagement, risking the kinds of trouble we have already seen at Johnson & Johnson, Boeing, Lothrop, and Northern Defense.

THE PATH FORWARD

Wait a minute! Is the goal of a culture transformation to make employees happy? So what if employees want to see their values reflected in the culture and feel frustrated by challenges such as blame and inconsistency? You might be thinking that what is really needed to improve performance is for these complaining employees and managers to just go back to work.

But stop and think about this from the perspective of your competitive advantage. Employees who embody the kinds of values found at the communal level of awareness present a rich opportunity. First, employees want to work at this level, and they want their organizations to operate at this level too. And the research has shown that organizations that do operate at this level are in fact high performing. From Kotter and Heskitt's research in the 1990s through Collins's and Porras's work, presented in *Built to Last*, we have been shown that firms with a strong adaptive culture based on shared values significantly outperform firms with rigid or weak cultures.[15]

What is different about these companies that outperform their peers? From the classic Collins and Porras research to *Fortune*'s annual list of Best Companies to Work For, there is a focus on how companies work. The high-performing and low-performing companies faced the same adversities, and all of them had reasonable strategies. The key differentiator is to face those challenges with the right people on board and a culture that permits those people to address challenges openly and collaboratively.

As Jim Collins states with some surprise in *Good to Great*: "Clearly the good-to-great companies did get incredible commitment and alignment—they artfully managed change—but they never really spent much time thinking about it. It was utterly transparent to them. We learned that under the right conditions, the problems of commitment, alignment, motivation, and change just melt away. They largely take care of themselves."[16] We have an interesting gap to cross. On one side of the chasm are the employees who would like to work in an environment in which their communal level of awareness values are supported. On the other side is the organization that needs its employees to operate at this level of awareness in order to work effectively and to be innovative and adaptive enough to meet new challenges and achieve the stated goals.

How do you build the bridge? How does your organization create an aligned culture that will help it reach its goals? It turns out that there is a logical flowchart for creating this alignment. The power values of integrity, commitment, and transparency define the steps your organization has to work through to align the values present in the three elements of its culture: the collective principles and beliefs of the organization and its employees, the collective mission and goals of the organization and its employees, and the collective standards of behavior:

- *Integrity.* The first step is to reduce any negativity in the organization to a level at which it does not interfere with the core business. When leaders throughout your company demonstrate and demand consistency and predictability in their conduct and in how the organization does its business, employees have fewer reasons to fall back on thinking only about their self-interest. With less confusion and inconsistency, it is easier for them to live out their communal level of awareness values, and they find fewer reasons to rationalize selfish behavior, deceive themselves that wrong is right, or simply disengage and let problems pass them by. Developing integrity will be a key element in creating organization-wide consistency and predictability by effectively linking your organization's standards of behavior (its proverbial "walk") to its mission and goals (its "talk").

- *Commitment.* The second step toward alignment is to ensure that engagement awareness is alive and well by creating an environment in which employees are willing to step up and take responsibility for their actions, in which they care enough to risk asking questions and then to contribute to the solutions. Organizations that understand what drives commitment will take steps to increase their employees' intrinsic motivation by giving them greater autonomy. Commitment

will link what is important to employees—their principles and beliefs—
to the organization's mission and goals.

  ○   *Transparency.* Building systems and processes that demand
transparency will ensure that communal awareness values can be lived
and that problems and challenges are raised, discussed, and resolved
in a manner consistent with employees' personal values. Channels to
ensure clarity in communication and assurances that the truth will be
heard will permit employees to see whether their principles and beliefs
are reflected in the organization's standards of behavior.

  In the chapters in Part Two, we look at how the power of integrity,
commitment, and transparency connects what organizations need
done with what employees most wish to do.

PART 2

The Power Values

Integrity Aligns Goals
and Standards

Consistency and Fairness:
Are individual goals at odds
with standards?

Accountability and Consequences:
Do people do what they say
they're going to do?

Logging and timber production have traditionally been among the most dangerous of industries. Beyond the hazards of felling trees, there are countless ways workers can be cut, crushed, or otherwise injured or killed. And yet Weyerhaeuser, one of the oldest and largest timber companies in the world, chose to emphasize its employee safety program by focusing on, of all things, seat belts. "It may seem strange that we even needed a program like this," said Richard Hanson, the former chief operating officer.[1] In the states where Weyerhaeuser operates, existing laws mandate wearing seat belts in all vehicles on the road. The expectations for compliance were clear. Nevertheless, the company decided to use seat belts to convey the message that it was serious about safety. Company leaders knew that the biggest challenge to any safety program is not the severity of the consequences for violation, but rather the consistency with which the policy is enforced—the more so since the company's workforce is mostly unionized. Weyerhaeuser employees drive a wide variety of vehicles, from big-rig logging trucks to forklifts, and in many job capacities, not all of them unionized, so insisting on seat belt safety gave Weyerhaeuser a way to demonstrate that safety was a standard to which everyone would be held accountable.

Weyerhaeuser's program had a simple name: "Unbuckled, Unsafe, Unemployed." As Hanson advised his people, "Please don't make the decision to be unemployed." A test of the company's seriousness came when two veteran workers with over thirty-five years of experience between them were caught driving a short distance in a company vehicle without their seat belts. When they were suspended for two months without pay, a loss of ten thousand dollars each, there was no pushback from the union. The point had been made.

I have worked with many companies in deploying ethics and compliance programs. What determines success is not just whether the standards are clearly articulated, but whether most employees believe that leadership takes those standards seriously. For example, two sales representatives at Western Financial were fired for forging customer information on insurance applications. They knew perfectly well they were breaking the rules, but they understood the practice to be widespread and never punished. In fact, the company had fired some sales reps for the same violation but had kept the firings hushed up. The sales reps were to blame for their own actions, which they knew to be wrong, but their leaders were to blame for creating the impression that Western Financial didn't take its own rules seriously.

In fact, when employees fall short of the rules, whether it is a logging safety precaution or an insurance underwriting procedure, it is rarely because they did not know what was expected of them. We generally know what the rules are. When we don't do what's expected of us, it's usually because we have made a decision not to. Ignoring a rule is often a social norm in itself. One of the typical responses my clients hear from wayward employees is something like, "I knew that procedure was on the books, but no one ever follows it." When we have—or seem to have—choices, we do a sophisticated real-time cost-benefit analysis of which rule, standard, or social norm to follow. And following the letter of the law or rigidly adhering to company policy may not be our first choice if the goal seems important enough, whether it's closing a sale or keeping (rather than firing) a valuable employee.

In some organizations, there is a prevailing presumption—whether true or not—that there are no consequences for not meeting a commitment to a colleague or the company. So if it's inconvenient or counter to one's self-interest to meet the commitment, then why should it be met? Other people weigh the benefits of doing something wrong against the odds of getting caught. But most of us wouldn't deliberately engage in misconduct even if we were sure we could get away with it. Instead, we balance our self-interest against our desire—at the communal level of awareness—to be a contributing member of a larger whole.

But precisely because level 5 values are so important to most of us, we can also be swayed by the organizational culture. We want to feel good about ourselves, and this is often based not only on our own moral codes but also on how we want others to perceive us. Even if an employee is considering a risky move because he selfishly wants to get ahead, he is also weighing how that decision would affect his social standing among his peers within the company. Depending on the culture around us, the need to fit in and be accepted can spur unproductive or risky behaviors. In particular, inconsistent norms and norms that are inconsistent with goals ("it's technically against the rules, but you're allowed to do it and it really works") can flip our mental switches for self-deception, rationalization, or disengagement. This seems to be what happened at Western Financial, and it happens every day in just about any organization when a goal can be accomplished at the expense of a standard—or a standard can be maintained at the expense of the underlying goal.

WHY INTEGRITY MATTERS

Integrity is the principle that one's words and actions should be consistent—one should do what one said one would do. Given that most employees seek out the communal level of awareness at work and are vulnerable to self-deception, rationalization, and disengagement, ensuring that your organization demonstrates integrity in how it conducts its business is at the heart of maintaining a high-performance culture. Western Financial's culture was lacking in integrity because the compliance rules said one thing and what was allowed was something else. In fact, there was a further violation of integrity in the fact that the company sometimes punished those who forged customer information and sometimes didn't. In other words, there was a goal of compliance, but the standards of behavior—how compliance was enforced—were inconsistent with the goal and even inconsistent with each other.

As the Western Financial example illustrates, integrity helps determine the extent to which employees will be willing to put aside self-interest for the benefit of the organization. For those sales reps, the personal success of making the sale outweighed the risk that noncompliance posed for the company—perhaps because the company itself didn't seem to take that risk very seriously. Conversely, lack of integrity determines the extent to which employees will feel that wrong is actually right or will feel unsure which of several options is the greater or lesser evil or will simply stop caring. Put another way, integrity helps prevent those mental switches for self-deception, rationalization, and disengagement from being switched on by social norms that are too much at variance with stated goals.

Recent research in behavioral economics has shown that how we perceive the threshold of acceptable behavior is a key factor in shaping whether we think what we are doing is right and honest. People, honest or not, do not live on a desert island. Honest people are more honest in an environment in which that value is upheld and are more inclined to cheat or do wrong if everyone else is doing it. Integrity becomes the foundation of a healthy culture because it sets the standard for the other standards we follow. Will the standards of behavior that the organization wants us to follow be consistent with the social norms that will actually guide what we do in our daily work? Integrity helps each of us define which social or organizational norms we accept and which we ignore.

People hate surprises at work. We like to know what we're getting into and want to get through a busy day without having to guess what mood the boss is in or what new changes in the schedule are going to be handed down after lunch. Even if things aren't perfect, we are more likely to be good team players when we know the rules of the game. It's much easier to fall into a habit of self-protection—at the company's expense, if necessary—when we are asked to contribute to the group without knowing what to expect in return. A lack of predictability and consistency can thwart culture alignment because it becomes too hard for people to align their individual motivations with a common set of goals.

The key slogan for integrity is not, "Do the right thing." It is, "Do what you say you're going to do." The enemy of integrity is not dishonesty or misconduct; it is inconsistency. Integrity is often defined as being synonymous with honesty, but with regard to creating a healthy organizational culture, the more applicable definition would be "the state of being whole, entire, or undiminished." Embedded in the concept of wholeness is the idea that all of the parts fit together. You don't have one set of values at home and a different set at work; you don't say one thing to one person and something different to someone else; you don't say you will do something and then blithely go on your way ignoring what you just said. It's less a matter of what the rules and standards are than a matter of whether we know how and if those rules will be applied. We need predictability to know what to expect and to decrease emotional stress—to know that logic and order characterize the system. Otherwise we need to spend extra energy defending what is ours rather than contributing to the benefit of the whole. Certainty and predictability are key foundations for trust, which, for our purposes, means that you can engage with a person or an organization without having to put your guard up. You can focus on the benefits of the relationship or interaction without having to dedicate time and energy to protecting yourself. As Roger Corbett, former CEO of Woolworths, Australia's largest supermarket chain, noted, "If a chief executive espouses one standard but lives another in his personal life and it is seen by the people in the business, then that moves the business further towards cynicism."[2]

INTEGRITY AND CULTURE

Developing integrity so that it is taken seriously as a value in a corporate culture is a challenge. Leaders can rightly insist that the members of the organization live the value of integrity, but they cannot will it into place merely by promulgating statements of core values or codes of conduct. The worthy concept of integrity must be painstakingly fashioned into a tangible reality, and this can be achieved only through effective processes, policies, and procedures. Consistency, by definition, is a quality that can be demonstrated only over time.

As a leader, you need to learn where your workforce is frustrated and pressured by inconsistency and then systematically remove those grounds for self-deception, rationalization, and disengagement. You must be aware of your own role in creating inconsistency and work on your own integrity first. An organization that creates consistency and predictability in how it does its business offers its employees a clear picture of what its goals are and the standards by which it expects employees to achieve those goals.

Of the 3 power values, integrity must be addressed first, before an organization can tackle commitment and transparency. An organization cannot credibly attempt to build high performance if it is still grappling with the negativity generated by inconsistent or unfair practices. Integrity is the means by which an organization can reduce that negativity by aligning its mission and goals with its standards of behavior. Having accomplished that, an organization may be able to generate employee commitment in part through transparency—ensuring that operations are transparent and that issues can be raised. But such positive attributes cannot be sustained without integrity in the nuts and bolts of the business's everyday operations. Inconsistency—lack of integrity—leads to frustrations in day-to-day work that will undermine commitment and transparency. In fact, inconsistency is one of the most often cited limiting values at the performance level of awareness.

How does a company systematically build integrity? A healthy culture is founded on how employees react to the ways the organization gets its work done. Embedded in this statement are three sets of questions the leader needs to ask:

1. *Are our organization's goals clear to employees?* Does every employee know what is expected of him or her? Do employees know how their personal goals and targets connect to the organization's broader goals?
2. *Is it clear to employees how our organization expects them to meet their goals?* Are standards of behavior well articulated, or is it up to everyone to decide for themselves what to do? How has the organization balanced its official standards and rules against the informal ways people go about their work day to day?
3. *Do our organization's leaders walk the talk?* Even if the goals for various projects and initiatives and the expected standards of behavior have been clearly stated, are they being followed? Do people do what they say they're going to do? And if not, what are the consequences?

The key to building integrity in any organization is to break the concept down into observable behaviors and actions that can be measured and therefore managed. As integrity links together an organization's goals and its standards of behavior, it is important to get a full sense of how you can take stock of these two elements of culture.

Mission and Goals

Many organizations have found it difficult to express their goals in terms of behaviors that people can actually act on. In many cases, the strategic objectives that senior leaders develop do not include articulated behaviors directly applicable to any particular employee. An employee might think, *"Bringing people together" may be a lovely corporate mission, but exactly what am I supposed to be doing right now that fits that description?* In addition, the organization's broader goals may not be consistent with the narrower goals that an individual employee pursues in his or her daily work. During a period of organizational change, for example, a particular employee's goal may be not to make waves—hardly a goal the corporate strategists have in mind.

Western Financial faced a challenge in defining goals for its top-performing sales representatives. The reps were compensated according to how much new business they brought in; they were responsible for the firm's top-line revenue. However, just because a new case was brought in did not mean that it was good for Western Financial. If underwriting standards were being violated, the company might be taking on too much risk, resulting in future payouts that would hurt the bottom line. Leadership therefore wanted sales representatives and underwriters to work together as a team, both for efficiency and to present a unified face to customers. However, because the sales representatives and the underwriters had quite different goals and incentives, there was an inherent tension in prioritizing work, even if the particular sales rep and underwriter had a cordial working relationship. A sales representative, for example, might have a chance to sign an exciting new prospect—if Western could change the eligibility requirements for a particular benefit. For the underwriting team, however, the goal wasn't to bring in new business; it was to ensure that new business was profitable. Each underwriter had risk metrics against which he or she would be evaluated. The underwriter's individual performance rating might take a hit for approving what was actually a worthwhile risk. In short, leadership demonstrated a lack of integrity by giving sales reps and underwriters the goal of working together for the good of the company while establishing standards of behavior that put the two groups at odds with each other.

As a leader, you need to be aware of how inherent conflicts like this weigh on employees' ability to do their jobs day in and day out, not to mention how they provoke people to try to game the system just so they can get something done. Organizations with healthy corporate cultures develop the means to identify such issues and then take corrective action in a way that allows employees to be part of the solution in aligning their own day-to-day work. When strategy becomes policy and policy becomes day-to-day behavior, individual employees need direction on how to manage inconsistencies between what they are asked to do and what they need to do, and they should be able to play their part in straightening these crooked lines.

Standards of Behavior

In all organizations, multiple rules and standards apply to any particular situation. There are broad codes of conduct and sets of business practices, plus operating procedures for each work group. Although it would be nice to think that each individual manager or employee can make a yes-or-no decision whether to adhere to any particular standard, it is of course much more complicated than that.

For example, I have worked for many years with a number of multinational corporations, many of which have bought and sold a variety of manufacturing facilities. It is not unusual for a twenty- or thirty-year veteran of a particular facility to have had three, four, or five different corporate logos on his or her paycheck. This makes for interesting answers when I ask what one would think would be a simple question: "What company do you work for?" While my client at "Acme" corporate headquarters would hope that each employee or manager would answer that he or she works for Acme, in many instances an employee's sense of identity and loyalty is to his or her particular facility. If that facility has been in business for many years, it has a slew of informal ways to do business that, in the mind of such an employee, transcends the facility's corporate ownership. It is truly "how *we* do things around *here*." If a large multinational acquires the facility and reorganizes it into a different business unit, there can easily be a jumble of standards or processes that would apply to any particular situation. I have been confronted by managers who ask me plaintively, "Do I follow corporate procedures, do I follow our business unit procedures, or do I follow the procedures that have worked well in this facility for the past twenty years?"

Matters can be even more complicated if there is a widespread perception that the way things have been done locally for twenty years is in fact the best way to do them. A decision coming out of a distant corporate office to change a process may be perceived locally as a decision made only to benefit a corporate objective that has never been explained or made relevant to the local workforce. One plant, for example, had always been able to custom-make its own parts; in a pinch, this could speed up throughput. After being bought, though, the plant was required to order parts through a centralized system. When a job was being held up to wait for a part on order that could actually be made right there, it could be hard indeed to know which standards should apply.

As a leader, it may be beyond your power to sort all this out entirely satisfactorily. The key, however, is to not let the workforce feel that no standards apply. Then all hell breaks loose. In many instances in which employees and managers face conflicting sets of standards and processes, they are left with the unstated expectation that they should do whatever they think best. In the wrong culture, this can open a Pandora's box of trouble. As you have already learned, our personal ethical standards do not exist in a vacuum. Our self-perception of honesty is partly dependent on knowing that external standards govern our behavior.

INTEGRITY ALIGNS GOALS AND STANDARDS

Integrity is the link that ensures that goals and standards are logically and deliberately related to one another. Standards of behavior can help ensure alignment of goals, and clarity of the goals themselves can help ensure consistent standards of behavior. We can look at the gap between goals and standards from the perspective of the organization and of an individual employee and manager. From each vantage point, we can see what is needed to close that gap.

Employees look at the actions of their coworkers and their leaders and want to know if those people's individual goals are at odds with the stated goals of the organization. Are leaders determining their own goals in contrast to the organization's declared goals? Are decisions made at a local or individual level in conflict with expected standards of behavior? Are actions being taken to meet someone's personal short-term objectives at the expense of longer-term commitments? If your people can see these things happening, they will sense unequal treatment or favoritism, which can make them feel justified in putting their own interests first. This becomes an issue of fairness and consistency.

An integrity-based culture is determined by how seriously the organization takes its commitments. Whether it's a corporate policy or a verbal commitment between two people or two teams, how serious is the commitment to do what you say you are going to do? Are there consequences for not doing what you say you are going to do? If the social norm of the organization (or the team) says that keeping your word is not sacrosanct, then the standards of behavior are not aligned with the goals. This is an issue people face every day. Let's say that you need information from Mary in order to finish an analysis you are going to present to senior leadership. Mary works in a different division but has promised to deliver her numbers to you on the date by which you need them. As that date passes, you cannot reach her by phone, and she doesn't respond to your urgent e-mails. The next day, your boss is angry at you for being late with the analysis, and you try Mary again. She answers the phone and, without apology or explanation, says she will get you the data as soon as she can. Are there consequences for her not living up to her commitments? This becomes an issue of accountability and responsibility.

These two dimensions of integrity—fairness and consistency, on the one hand, and accountability and responsibility, on the other—can do the most to mitigate the risks generated by fear and frustration at the first three levels of awareness: survival, relationship, and performance.

Fairness and Consistency from the Employee's Point of View

How employees see the goals of the organization is often quite different from the assumptions made at corporate headquarters. The fairness and consistency of those goals and objectives play a prominent role in shaping employees' perceptions of their organization's culture. For a leader, having a sense of how your actions are perceived in the field is a critical first step to establishing true integrity.

Fairness

What happens when there are exceptions to the rules? What happens when a manager or leader operates by his or her own set of rules? What happens when some employees work toward one set of goals but a perceived favorite group or individual works toward a different set? Such circumstances make it difficult to have alignment between standards and goals because what is happening just isn't fair, and fairness is critical: it is a key communal awareness value. People expect it in themselves and in others. We have cared about fairness and aspired to it since we were children. In most Western cultures, people seek a level playing field, where we at least believe that anyone can succeed. This is especially true for Americans. A core part of the American culture is that anyone, given the opportunity and unhindered by institutional or societal barriers, can achieve at least some level of success.

In organizations that conduct values assessments, it is common for employees to identify fairness as a personal value in circumstances in which fairness is being challenged. It is almost as if employees feel the need to broadcast to the organization that fairness is a critical personal value as a way of calling attention to the perceived lack of fairness in the work environment. It is perhaps also a reminder to their leaders that the employees consider fairness to be a critical value for a high-performing organization.

From my experience working with organizations addressing ethics and culture challenges, fairness is often the pivot point that will determine if an organization is going to move toward culture alignment or continue down the slippery slope toward dysfunction. People will normally be open and willing to contribute—even sacrifice—for the benefit of the whole as long as they perceive that they are being treated fairly. No one likes a pay cut, but people will accept one as long as it applies to everybody—from top to bottom. Once people perceive that they are being treated unfairly—for example, noticing that the company's talk about work/life balance means that salaried employees get time off to take their kids to the doctor but hourly employees do not—they turn 180 degrees and focus on protecting their own self-interest. This can often lead to self-deception, rationalization, and disengagement—all harbingers of lower organizational performance, and possibly worse.

Research has shown a paradoxical relationship between fairness and cheating. Often our very concern with fairness leads us to cut corners in the first place. If we see ourselves being treated unfairly, then inappropriate, unethical, or even illegal actions appear to be a necessary—and therefore legitimate—way to even the score.[3] Some research has shown that a certain amount of low-level cheating is in fact natural. Some even claim that it can be a productive response—our brain's way of seeking shortcuts to meet goals.

The good news, however, is that our natural inclination for shortcuts is balanced by a willingness to follow rules that we accept as fair, even if we have an opportunity and an incentive to break them. Therefore, the credibility of a standard—the integrity with which it is aligned, observed, and enforced—makes the standard able to help us balance our personal definition of fairness with our commitment to the organization's common good. This catalytic or enabling quality makes integrity one of the power values.

We always walk a fine line when it comes to fairness. It should not exist at the expense of employees' being assertive and taking reasonable risks. We learn at an early stage to compete and to compare ourselves to others. Getting into good schools and getting ahead at work require careful strategy and planning; we want to gain whatever edge we can to get ahead. How do we know when we have gone too far—or are about to do so? When are we taking unfair advantage of another, and when are we cheating ourselves by being too unassertive?

The introduction to self-deception in Chapter One noted that once we start cheating or treating others unfairly, it becomes easier to impute that behavior to others. A common excuse I hear when I ask people why they speed on the highway is, "Everyone else is doing it." Once we see our own cheating as a response to someone else's cheating—for example, taking credit for another's work in order to advance to a position we feel we have been cheated out of—it becomes hard to stop. We begin to convince ourselves that we are entitled to the success, that it really is due to our innate abilities. Cheating can also be intended as a protection against failure. Especially in sales and finance, no one wants to be seen as having been duped or as not being the most successful.

In large organizations, employees—whether managers or hourly machine operators—interact with a variety of people every day. Their determination of their own accomplishment or success is often based on informal comparisons with others. Hourly employees might compare themselves to other employees on different teams working under different supervisors; those working the day shift might compare themselves to the night shift. A very common source of frustration is that some other employees are seen as getting some special privilege. And this is where one takes the first steps toward rationalization.

Why is unfairness so dangerous? Because people in every organization have frustrations. The question is whether those frustrations can turn employees against their organization. When an individual or a group has crossed the line and no longer looks out for the organization's best interests first, the risks to the organization increase. Such employees—and it may be a whole workforce—are no longer as engaged and productive, and they may in fact be thinking of ways to get back from the company what they think they deserve. It's the start of the slippery slope toward rationalizing misbehavior: "I deserve this unfair advantage since no one recognizes my true contribution." The response can go as far as revenge in the form of a sit-down strike or even sabotage.

Also, most organizations expect and encourage employees to "do more with less." Leaders at all levels hope for high levels of personal responsibility; they want the people working under them to take on more challenges, assume more responsibility, and do what it takes to get the job done right. This is very difficult to expect when people feel that they are being treated unfairly.

Sometimes unfairness is an institutional problem. For example, when an organization has established best practices for particular processes and procedures but then skimps on those best practices because of budget or scheduling pressures, it creates confusion and sometimes the perception of unfairness.

Perceptions of unfairness can also be linked to perceptions of favoritism. Many frontline supervisors rely on friends and people they know well because they know those people will do the job. Others who are not part of the supervisor's social group can easily feel ostracized, which sets up a negative cycle in which those on the outside come to see all decisions in the context of unfairness.

Consistency

Inconsistency is the most frequently reported negative value at the performance level of awareness. It strongly influences employees' views on how well the organization does its business, that is, how well it performs. Consistency and predictability are therefore the antidotes to many of the challenges most organizations face at level 3 relating to limiting values such as inconsistency and confusion. Most employees I have worked with are incredibly resilient. They can put up with just about anything that management throws at them. But don't surprise them. People want to know what they are up against; known challenges are always easier to handle than the unknown ones. Inconsistency drives people crazy because they have to analyze and evaluate every action or statement for its underlying meaning, and it can become exhausting. Building systems that are consistent and predictable—that is, developing the power value of integrity—permits employees to gauge expectations and then develop whatever internal coping mechanisms they may need to make even an imperfect system work as well as it can.

Creating consistency in standards and in goals is necessary but not necessarily easy. Even organizational successes can create crises of integrity. For example, organizations often grow through acquisition or evolve organically through stages, ending up with a hodgepodge of standards that may be permitting inconsistent social norms to flourish. Mergers, acquisitions, or bouts of rapid hiring can result in unstable and risky mixtures of cultures, whether from different entities that have been brought together or from people who joined the organization before and after some organizational turning point.

I worked with a pharmaceutical company, which I will call PharmX, which started as a small venture-backed research and development firm in the 1990s. By the mid-2000s, it had grown into a large manufacturer and distributor, largely through a series of acquisitions. Employees in acquired facilities in Denver and Milwaukee still revered their original corporate identities and cultures. They accepted at face value PharmX's promises that once their businesses were acquired, they would be left alone to operate independently. But as PharmX grew, its corporate goals were not seen as being the same as the goals for the Denver and Milwaukee locations. As a result, managers in these facilities had trouble knowing how to prioritize their time and efforts, which reduced their effectiveness and efficiency.

Each plant, each function, and each cohort of employees seemed to have its own culture, and there was no view of a common PharmX culture. While it is common to have multiple views of a company's culture, the extent of the variation at PharmX may have been an indication that leadership had not yet articulated a unified vision of the company's future, leaving each employee to fall back on his or her own perceptions.

The vacuum created by leadership's inability to forge an integrated culture made it difficult for any one employee or manager to know which rules or even social norms applied in any particular situation. More aggressive managers took matters into their own hands and made risky decisions that got the company into significant trouble with the U.S. Food and Drug Administration for off-label marketing.[4]

How did it happen? No one I interviewed ever suggested that any individual or group had maliciously intended to commit fraud—for personal gain or otherwise. Instead, some managers pushed the envelope, only to find that the envelope didn't resist, allowing them to cross the line into misconduct. There was no counterbalance to hold back aggressive strategies and plans that some felt were necessary to keep the organization competitive. Some told me that sales reps felt that marketing never provided all the data they needed to support the product claims, while marketing felt that sales reps were taking the lack of clarity on product descriptions and parameters as a green light to go beyond acceptable promotional claims in order to meet aggressive sales goals. Others pointed out that the sales, marketing, and medical affairs functions were not working together to implement the directives they received from senior management.

One way or another, top management's toleration of inconsistency had finally led to severe problems. Inconsistency provided cover for managers to selectively hear and choose which standards they would follow, allowing them to create a crooked path that they used to justify their actions. It is no different than what we learned as children in selectively turning mom's qualified permission to do something into a full-blown okay when dad asked us if mom agreed to whatever plot we were cooking up.

Accountability and Consequences from the Organization's Point of View

Integrity in a culture hinges on whether the organization's leadership takes seriously the concept of "do what you say you're going to do." Employees look to see whether there are consequences for not living up to their commitments. What they see will dramatically affect their commitment to the organization's goals.

Accountability

Problems with inconsistency and unfairness naturally lead to questions of accountability. What, if anything, happens when someone doesn't do what he or she is supposed to do? When I work with leaders trying to prioritize which values will make their organization high performing, we often come back to accountability. As one CEO told me, "The only value that matters is: 'Live up to your commitments.' Everything else is secondary." If the mission statement of his organization had simply been, "We do what we say we're going to do," he would have been happy.

In interviews with employees, supervisors, and even directors and vice presidents, the same issue emerges: employees want their leaders to lead. They want their managers to have the authority to make decisions that affect their work group, and they want those managers to step up and make those decisions. Nothing frustrates employees more than having critical matters sit undecided because a leader, often off-site, hasn't gotten around to making a decision.

This frustration comes through loud and clear in values assessments. When employees express fear for their jobs or for the company's viability, they are looking for help. They want their leaders to take charge and make things better. When such fears are unaddressed, it is hard to get much traction on anything as broad and conceptual as integrity. Employees in such circumstances need good information from leaders whom they respect and trust. When there is bad news, employees want straight talk. Leaders are often tempted to sugarcoat information, fearful of exacerbating uncertainty. But employees, however low their position in the hierarchy, are not children. Most of them are parents or caregivers, used to taking on responsibility and dealing with challenges. They know that there is no such thing as permanent job security. All they want is the truth.

Accountability is the antidote to the challenges at the performance level of awareness connected to bureaucracy. So much of the confusion and frustration of dealing with bureaucracy can be cleared away when employees are confident that leadership will make firm decisions to guide the organization. In most instances, employees are not asking for the power to make the decisions themselves. Values assessments are not openings for mutiny or for democratization of the workplace. Employees, whatever their level, just want their leaders to make decisions.

This was certainly the case at PharmX. During my interviews with employees and frontline managers, I heard a recurring theme: "Either make the decision, or empower local leadership to make the decision." Employees resented the fact that their own local leaders were not able to make local decisions. To them, it felt as if headquarters considered the entire facility untrustworthy. Still, if decisions must be made from a central headquarters, then at least empower—and require—someone at headquarters to make them.

Recall that Jim McNerney recognized this problem at Boeing when he chastised managers for "hiding in the bureaucracy." He understood that employees want their leaders to lead, to do what they implicitly said they would do simply by accepting their positions as leaders. Most employees would welcome a clear no—preferably accompanied by an explanation of why not—to, "We'll see." This problem at the performance level of awareness makes it harder for people to do their jobs; they never know what the decision is going to be, and they have to waste time trying to get an answer rather than getting something useful done for a customer.

Accountability in Teams

Many organizations have multiple locations and multiple business units that need to coordinate with each other and with centralized support functions. In this matrix of reporting responsibilities, employees and managers working on projects commonly have dotted-line reporting responsibilities to managers who are not their bosses. In these situations, effective teamwork is a must, and that requires accountability, which is the organization's enforcement of individual integrity: "Do what you said you were going to do, or this is what happens to you."

People I met in PharmX's R&D facility in New Jersey, for example, enjoyed working in teams and saw healthy teamwork as critical to their success. When staffing was short, for example, employees pulled together to ensure that the job got done. Yet the success of these teams at the small group level broke down when PharmX created larger interdepartmental teams. One reason was a perceived lack of accountability. Team members lacked the natural cohesion and loyalty of all being in the same department, so it was much easier for some members to slack off. There were no "sticks" for these nonperformers, which was "really irritating" and ultimately demoralizing for other team members, who saw their team's performance standards sink to a lowest-common-denominator level. When I addressed these issues with senior leaders, I discovered that they themselves were undermining their employees' commitments to interdepartmental teams. They were always calling their own people back from the team to their own group and were not granting them the time and resources to meet their interdepartmental team commitments.

PharmX's leadership faced a serious integrity challenge of aligning the goal of teamwork with the standards applied to team participation. If teams were important to the organization (they certainly were important to these communal-awareness-level employees), leadership had to grant the teams the authority to do what they were chartered to do. This required a clear and overt change in leadership's own conduct. Accountability was the key to teamwork.

Consequences

If an organization is to have accountability, consequences must be in place for not aligning one's actions with the stated goals. If there are no consequences for not adhering to standards, the standards have no meaning.

Leaders at Western Financial, for example, couldn't understand why certain successful, high-potential sales representatives had committed fraud by misrepresenting critical data to the underwriters in order to have their clients' cases approved. At first, both the company leadership and I suspected that these sales reps were desperate to meet aggressive sales quotas. But in fact, they had already met their goals. Something else was driving their behavior. It turned out that one of the primary factors was their perception of a lack of consequences for their actions. These were competitive people with strong egos, and they needed to succeed. Getting an "impossible" case through underwriting was a feather in their cap, something they could boast about to their colleagues. They had noticed that the organization did not seem to punish small infractions; it seemed to them either that management and internal audit were incompetent or that they themselves were better sales reps than the rest. With little respect for the rules, they found themselves on their way down the slippery slope.

As I pointed out earlier, these reps had been mistaken. Other employees had been terminated for misconduct, but this had never been publicized to the workforce. The compliance department's low-profile approach had created the impression that nobody seemed to care. Consequences matter, and certainly the apparent lack of consequences mattered at Western Financial. When someone gets away with something, that gets around through the grapevine quickly. Finding a way, within the boundaries of confidentiality, to publicize that employees have had to face the consequences for violations of standards is a powerful demonstration that the organization takes these issues seriously.

Taking Steps to Instill Integrity

Fairness, consistency, and accountability issues run deep in the frustrations and challenges facing employees and managers. You need to understand the source of these perceptions if you hope to build integrity. Acknowledging and addressing areas of inconsistency will do a lot to mitigate the negative impact when employees are frustrated at the first two levels of awareness: survival and relationship. When evaluating the extent of the fairness and consistency issues in your company, look for the root causes for your employees' perceptions of unfairness and inconsistency. This will help you decide how to target those areas more directly.

In evaluating root causes, it can be helpful to look back on the seven levels of awareness. If employees feel threatened at the levels of survival, self-image, and self-esteem, more sophisticated issues will be seen as nonessential.

Level 1: Survival Awareness

Anxieties at the survival level of awareness are often reflected in employees' perceptions that their leaders are concerned only with next quarter's results. On values assessments, "excessive focus on the bottom line" and "short-term focus" are often the most common values chosen at this foundational level of awareness. To create a dynamic culture of performance, the organization must address the impact its focus on quarterly results has on integrity. In many organizations I have worked with, the long-term growth policies are actually inconsistent with short-term exigencies. In one organization, for example, employees had been promised a certain level of employee development in the form of training courses, conference attendance, and even travel to corporate offices. Local supervisors insisted that employee development is critical for nurturing enthusiasm and motivation. All the same, as soon as there were serious budget challenges, those employee development programs were the first line items to be cut.

Employees understood the financial challenges their organization was facing, but they resented the fact that no leader had been willing to step up and help reconcile these two conflicting goals: employee development and short-term budget concerns. Employees were seeking an open and honest conversation on how leadership expected to straddle these conflicting priorities—they were seeking accountability for what needed to be done—but all they got were evasive noncommittal statements.

In another organization I recently worked with, employees expressed a pervasive desire to know that their supervisors were "watching their backs." Certainly a manager cannot create job security or save the plant, but he or she can reduce fear by demonstrating that employees will be kept informed and not left in the dark. Often it takes no more than simply acknowledging that the employee is a living, breathing human being by saying "hello" or "good morning" at the beginning of a shift, yet many employees cannot even count on this. From their point of view, a boss whose goal, by definition, includes looking out for his or her employees but cannot adhere to even a standard of basic politeness is hardly a beacon of the organization's integrity.

In other organizations, knowing that a supervisor is "watching my back" would call for supervisors to provide their people with informal coaching on how to navigate the inconsistencies that employees face. Instead, many employees see their supervisors "kicking the can down the road" and refusing to take ownership of these vexing issues.

Level 2: Relationship Awareness

In many organizations, blame and disrespect are critical obstacles for employees who are trying to navigate between standards and goals. Maintaining open communication and positive interpersonal relationships is not easy. One of the values employees choose to describe their work environment is "empire building." Flaunting corporate policies— possibly taking advantage of weak corporate leadership—a tough supervisor might tell his or her people, "The only rules that matter are my rules." Of course, this makes it difficult to have consistent companywide practices and creates stress on several levels. Employees often feel that such a supervisor makes it tough for them to take advantage of development or promotional opportunities across the organization or seek redress by going to corporate.

The remedy for local tyranny is consistency. Strong systems and processes that govern behavior across the organization make it difficult for local managers to engage in behaviors that are inconsistent with stated norms. Even if a leader is not seen as a tyrant, dealing with the pressure and influence of peers and supervisors can create tension when employees cannot tell whose rules and standards apply.

This story is based on an incident that occurred at a company I'll call Carson Manufacturing, a venerable manufacturing company that had been founded well before the incorporation of its current corporate owner. In fact, some employees are third-generation workers at the facility. The company had just landed a new contract and was hiring new staff. A new part-timer, Mike, was eager to learn the ropes in hopes of landing a full-time position. Paul, who had been with the company for twenty-five years, was assigned to show Mike how to operate the grinding processor. To prove to "the kid" that he was a good guy, Paul showed him some tricks of the trade, including a quick way to clean out the unit when it became clogged with filings. The trick was to use a side panel so that it wasn't necessary to shut the whole unit down.

Later in his first week, Mike attended a safety briefing given by Steve, the new safety manager. Steve demonstrated how to use the equipment, including the new guard that had been installed on the grinding processor in response to a new standard promulgated by the Occupational Safety and Health Administration (OSHA). Mike quickly realized that Paul was not following these procedures, and he could see why: the safety guard blocked the side panel that Paul found so useful for unclogging the unit.

In fact, Paul and his supervisor, Richard, had been griping about this guard ever since Steve had had it installed. The guard made it trickier and slower to operate the grinding processor, and removing and reattaching the guard to unclog the machine took considerable time. Richard knew that if all his workers used the guard as they were supposed to, they would not meet their production numbers and would receive no bonus money. Besides, no one had been hurt using the machine in the twenty years before the guard was mandated. Richard had argued with Steve over this, and everyone knew how Richard felt about it.

Returning from the safety training, Mike pulled Richard aside and asked him what he should do about the guard: Use it or ignore it? Richard told Mike in a loud voice that everyone, including Paul, could hear, "Of course, you should use the guard. That's the rule." Richard then gave Paul a wink and sent Mike back to his station.

But Mike was trying to learn the ropes and hoping to fit in as quickly as possible, so he followed Paul's example and didn't use the guard. One day, because he was inexperienced, he let a piece of metal become pinched between the back of the unit and the grinding wheel. A shard of metal shot out of the machine like a bullet and took out a chunk of wall. Anyone standing nearby could have been killed. When Steve arrived on the scene, he found Richard disciplining Mike for not following proper procedures.

What should Mike have done? Could a newcomer really have been expected to follow a rule that everyone around him was ignoring? The more important question is, What should Richard and Steve have done?

As strategy filters down to policy, which filters down to your people's on-the-job behavior, you have a responsibility to make sure standards of behavior are clear and aligned as well as possible with goals—in other words, you need to maintain integrity. Steve and Richard both came up short in this regard. Steve's goal was to ensure safety, but in fact, he never made sure that Richard aligned the standards in his department with that goal. Nor did he try to find a better way to ensure safety without impeding performance. Had he done either one, Mike would never have been put in the position he was in. Richard had both production and safety goals, but he let one override the other rather than try to find a way to reconcile them. Nor was his goal of leading his group aligned with his actual practice of letting Paul do as he saw fit, even in violation of OSHA regulations. In short, Steve needed to be held accountable for walking the talk—making sure the rules were followed; Richard needed to be held accountable for walking his own talk—balancing production and safety and supervising his supervisees rather than letting one of them get another into serious trouble.

As a leader in your own organization, you can ensure that integrity is taken seriously in these ways:

- Hold your people responsible for how their actions and their omissions affect those around them. Otherwise it is difficult for integrity to be taken seriously. Individual actions will dominate, and alignment of the culture will be overwhelmed by the actions of strong individuals like Paul.
- Hold yourself responsible in the same way. You may need to gather feedback on how your own actions and omissions are affecting others in ways you did not intend.

Remember that for your people, informal social norms can be just as important as written standards of behavior, and maybe more important. Understanding where social norms conflict with other standards and being able to set clear guidelines is a critical step in ensuring fairness and consistency.

At first it may seem like a paradox, but integrity is often stronger in organizations that focus more on the small stuff than on making a big splash with integrity as a stated value. When employees see the leaders of the organization acting consistently and predictably and know their leaders' actions are fair and logical, they will see that integrity is taken seriously. There's no need to start big with a value like integrity. Small steps in which actions can speak louder than words will have dramatic ripple effects throughout the organization.

Commitment Aligns
Principles and Goals

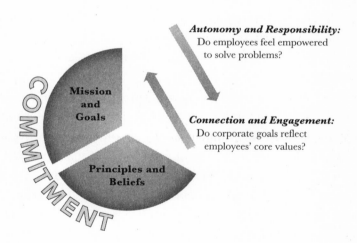

Autonomy and Responsibility:
Do employees feel empowered
to solve problems?

Connection and Engagement:
Do corporate goals reflect
employees' core values?

**Mission
and
Goals**

**Principles and
Beliefs**

COMMITMENT

At a staff meeting the day before Hurricane Katrina hit the U.S.
Gulf Coast in summer 2005, Walmart CEO Lee Scott declared,
"This company will respond to the level of this disaster. A lot of you
are going to have to make decisions above your level. Make the best
decision that you can with the information that's available to you at

the time and, above all, do the right thing."[1] This edict was passed down to the store managers with the expectation that this would be how the situation would be handled.

More than 170 Walmart facilities in Louisiana, Mississippi, Florida, and Alabama were affected by Katrina; 126 stores were closed due to damage or power outages. Some twenty thousand associates and their families were affected in some way. As the storm hit Mississippi, a Walmart store just a stone's throw from the coast was engulfed by a storm-driven wave estimated at thirty feet. Assistant manager Jessica Lewis, shocked by the devastation experienced by neighbors and long-time customers, decided to salvage what she could. Although she couldn't reach Walmart's emergency operations center or any of her superiors to get approval, she and her stepbrother ran a small bulldozer through the ruined store, loading it with shoes, clothes, and other items that hadn't been destroyed by the surge of water. She piled them in the parking lot and began giving them away to anyone in need. When a police chief and a local hospital representative appealed to Lewis, saying they were running short of critical drugs, she broke into the store's locked pharmacy.[2]

Walmart regional manager Ronny Hayes, in Kenner, Louisiana, said, "When I went in initially, I was thinking I need to determine the damage to our stores and find out what's the situation with our associates. But after being there for a couple of hours, it totally shifted from that to, 'Oh my God, what can we do to help these people?'" According to a study of Walmart's response to Katrina undertaken by the Kennedy School of Government, Hayes asked the local sheriff to accompany him to the store. Hayes told the police that if they could secure the store from looting, the officers could take what they needed from the store. "I don't think anybody was worried about being paid for anything."[3]

Managers in areas that were not at the heart of the destruction did what they could to reopen their stores. Janie McNeil was a district manager who was unable to reach stores under her command in the New Orleans area. But on the day after the storm, she and a few associates began repairing and cleaning out the store in Slidell, which was without power. "As they worked, McNeil recalls, a steady stream of residents came to the door, anxiously asking when the store would open. McNeil and the others began handing out diapers, water, formula, and ice. Over the next couple of days, residents and dozens of police officers and firefighters came by for food, sleeping bags, toiletries, socks, and underwear. Some customers paid cash, but for most of the first responders, McNeil adopted a crude credit system, tallying purchases on slips of paper that the buyers then signed."[4]

Walmart leadership was praised for giving its managers the discretion to make real-time decisions in the midst of the crisis. The managers themselves were praised for their autonomy and for taking independent actions. Walmart leadership had recognized that only the local managers would have a good sense of the needs of their local communities. These managers took initiative and risks without worrying about whether they needed to get permission from senior leaders.

Even in the midst of a crisis, it took courage for these managers to make these decisions. Only people with confidence in both their own ability and the support of their management would have risked jeopardizing their jobs or their employer's property. In other circumstances, someone at the level of a store manager—even faced with disaster—would have insisted on getting authority from a higher-up before acting or would have waited for government officials to take responsibility.

Everyone wants to do what he or she feels is right, but many employees do not always feel free to do so in their capacity as employees; that is the hallmark of an organization's lack of commitment, the power value that links an organization's principles and beliefs to its mission and goals, whatever those goals might be. Although these particular circumstances were extraordinary, engaged employees acted autonomously in both day-to-day operations and faced more ordinary difficulties such as a disappointed customer or a missed shipment from a supplier. These are the cornerstones of commitment.

WHY COMMITMENT MATTERS

In this age of knowledge workers, organizations need their employees to be fully engaged and committed to their work and to the organization. It is not enough for employees to show up for work and do the minimum. You need them to be problem solvers, responsible for the areas they control. You need their heads and their hearts. A company's intangible capabilities, such as innovating and reacting to quickly changing market conditions, depend on employees and leaders who make the extra effort. An organization with a culture that encourages high-performing employees to make the extra effort has done its homework in creating an environment in which employees can live their values at work and feel confident that the organization trusts them to do the best job possible. An organization that has achieved this has successfully aligned its mission and goals with the principles and beliefs of its employees. To do that, the organization has fully developed the power value of commitment.

At first it might seem like a paradox: the more an organization encourages its employees to be aware of their own abilities—and, in fact, be able to work independently to the fullest of their abilities—the more integrated and aligned its culture can be. One might have thought the opposite: that an aligned culture must be a cultlike culture in which everyone thinks the same. But today's organizations are complex. Employees all know that only by having everyone working well together can the job get done. To do that, each employee must be aware of his or her role and be granted as much responsibility and ownership for the execution of that role as possible. This builds commitment and creates a culture in which people can operate to their fullest capabilities.

Leaders like this. They seek committed employees. Whether it's called "intellectual capital" or "the right people on the bus," companies need to make sure they have the right employees and then tap into the potential within each to maintain a competitive edge. Innovation and productivity are the by-products of having employees who care and are willing to go above and beyond the basics. Leaner organizations have fewer layers of management and need all of their employees to be more self-managing. This is the only way for companies to respond quickly enough to their ever-changing markets. Companies need employees to think of new ways to succeed and to take ownership of their own domains within the organization.

Commitment is also essential in managing risks. From ethics to safety to quality, leaders want employees and managers to take on greater levels of personal responsibility and accountability. Companies can't watch every action; they need employees to be self-policing and willing to take the initiative to report or act on what they observe. Employees won't do that if they're not engaged and don't feel committed to the organization.

Employees also seek commitment. A critical determinant of whether an organization has achieved an aligned and integrated culture is whether the people who work there feel an emotional commitment to the organization. Employees want to feel good about what they do all day. If they are being asked to work long hours and make work the prime focus of their creative energy, they want to feel good about that work. They need to believe in what the organization is doing, and they need to see their own roles in the organization clearly. When employees have that emotional connection, their natural human inclination to forgive and be flexible comes out. They are more likely to ignore the rough spots in how the organization does its work. They forgive the minor inconsistencies in policies and the personality flaws of their managers. But when employees do not feel connected, they can fall back on looking out only for themselves. When that happens, every bump in the road becomes a source of contention.

A strong lesson in commitment comes from fabled investor Warren Buffett. In his 2011 letter to shareholders, Buffett wrote:

> Our final advantage is the hard-to-duplicate culture that permeates Berkshire. And in businesses, culture counts.

To start with, the directors who represent you think and act like owners. They receive token compensation: no options, no restricted stock and, for that matter, virtually no cash. We do not provide them directors and officers liability insurance, a given at almost every other large public company. If they mess up with your money, they will lose their money as well. Leaving my holdings aside, directors and their families own Berkshire shares worth more than $3 billion. Our directors, therefore, monitor Berkshire's actions and results with keen interest and an owner's eye. You and I are lucky to have them as stewards.

This same owner-orientation prevails among our managers. In many cases, these are people who have sought out Berkshire as an acquirer for a business that they and their families have long owned. They came to us with an owner's mindset, and we provide an environment that encourages them to retain it. Having managers who love their businesses is no small advantage.

What are the consequences of not maintaining high levels of commitment?[5]

Chapter Three discussed the potential of organizations that maintain a high level of engagement awareness. Employees who feel a deep sense of engagement are willing to step up and ask questions because they care. From an ethics and compliance perspective, these employees are not afraid to report misconduct. Research has shown that employees with greater levels of commitment to their manager and company are less susceptible to misconduct than employees whose primary commitment is to their personal success. For example, sales representatives and others who are primarily compensated by commission or through discretionary bonuses have an obvious potential conflict of interest—a strong motivation to put their own interests ahead of the organization's. Without a well-developed sense of commitment to the welfare of the organization, such employees pose a higher risk of cutting corners on customer service or even management guidelines if it affects their compensation.[6] According to a survey of eighteen hundred employees in global organizations conducted by the Corporate Executive Board, a greater commitment to one's job than to the company and a high percentage of variable compensation were among the top five leading indicators of misconduct.

FOUNDATIONS OF COMMITMENT

Employees want to feel connected and committed to their companies, and leaders want their employees to step up and be willing and able to make decisions and take responsibility for their actions. It sounds like a win-win situation. Yet instilling commitment is a challenge for many companies. Perhaps it's because leaders don't know where to begin.

How do organizations begin the process of building commitment? Let's start by imagining an organization that seemingly lacks real commitment on the part of its employees. People come to work but are not very motivated. They watch the clock and never seem to go beyond the minimum that's expected of them. Relations between employees and managers are not hostile, but neither are they warm. Leadership can't think of any way to inspire employees that doesn't seem to come right out of *Dilbert*.

Yet I know from my work with organizations that even disgruntled employees in what seem to be the most dysfunctional cultures demonstrate some commitment. Most people develop strong relationships with their immediate coworkers. In many organizations that I have worked with, even if there are hostile relations between management and a unionized workforce or among various groups of employees, there is often a sense of commitment to one's immediate colleagues. Many people seek and benefit from the concept of a work family. They feel a sense of belonging and connection and demonstrate a sincere sense of personal responsibility toward the members of that "family." In other words, even in a dysfunctional organization, it is doubtful that the organization's problems are being caused by dysfunctional people.

So now we have a place to start from. We know from values assessments that employees in all types of organizations have communal awareness values. Employees may dislike their leadership or even their plant manager, but they demonstrate a strong commitment to their peers and the people they know personally. The organization's challenge, then, is to expand that sense of commitment found within that inner circle to the wider circles of colleagues and coworkers throughout the organization.

How does an organization begin that process? In addition to ensuring the integrity discussed in Chapter Four—that is, ensuring that employees at all levels do what they say they are going to do—the organization needs to tap into the natural desire to be a valued member of one's team and take personal responsibility for one's work. This means creating alignment between what the employees stand for— their principles and beliefs—and what the organization seeks to achieve—its mission and goals.

COMMITMENT ALIGNS PRINCIPLES AND GOALS

The interplay of commitment and culture is a two-way street. Employees would like to bring their full selves to work and know that what they stand for is consistent with the organization's goals and the principles and beliefs that the organization feels are necessary to achieve those goals. These employees, guided by their communal awareness values, are looking for a sense of belonging and connectedness. They want to feel a deep connection with the organization's purpose. It's even better if the organization's goals are exciting and generate passion. From the other side, leaders are looking to see if the employees' core values are in sync with the organization's objectives and goals. If so, the workforce can be counted on to assume greater levels of personal responsibility.

How does an organization align principles and goals? As a leader, you first need to understand just what principles and beliefs your employees have. Principles and beliefs are the personal core values that your people would like to see respected and encouraged at work. As you begin to engage employees in the process of discovering who they are and what they stand for, their perceptions of the organization and your perceptions of them will begin to change. New levels of understanding encourage greater levels of inclusiveness and a sense of belonging and connection. For example, as people begin to see how they could work together to get something done or get it done better, they start thinking more like owners (the good news), which means they can become more demanding of change to make that vision happen (the challenge). Later in this chapter, we explore how to increase that sense of connection.

Leaders must then develop the means to ensure that employees stay engaged. As you will see, one of the most effective ways is to give them as much independent responsibility as possible to develop their own plans of action. Engaged employees frequently cite greater autonomy as one of the most important reasons they like their work.

Issues that faced Western Financial's leadership highlight the challenges of aligning goals and principles to create a high-performing culture. Western Financial had a track record of success. It was clear to everyone, from the sales representatives to the back-office personnel, that the organization's primary goal was winning. "Failure is not an option" was the well-known mantra of Western's charismatic CEO. Less clear, however, was how the organization could exceed its previous record year after year. There was tremendous pressure on the sales representatives to bring in as much new business as possible (top-line revenue). However, back-office staff were concerned that the rush to bring in just any new business without proper underwriting would eventually reduce bottom-line revenue through increased payouts on claims. There was also a strong fear throughout the organization of what would happen if the annual goal were not met. "Two years of not meeting goals and you are out," was the common perception. Since more than half of the sales representatives had not made goal in the past two years, everyone in the organization felt tremendous pressure.

In addition, Western Financial's parent company had recently been reorganized. Western's CEO now had to answer more directly to the global leadership team, and new corporate policies and initiatives were making their way into Western's goals and planning. The glare of Western Financial's charismatic leader was now being clouded by new policies coming from senior leaders in a distant corporate headquarters with whom Western's employees had no personal connection.

What actually drove the employees at Western Financial? In the values assessment, they articulated a strong need to be appreciated and recognized. They sought opportunities to take ownership of their particular areas of expertise or responsibility. They also very much wanted to feel that they were making a difference to their customers. Within the organization, they needed to feel included. As the organization grew, it became harder to feel deeply connected to the leadership team. As the parent corporation's goals became more ambitious and complex, Western's employees were being pushed out of their comfort zones. They were willing to try, but they needed to know that their leaders were watching their backs.

How could leadership connect the aggressive goals of the organization with the strong desire of the employees to feel connected and valued? The first area to explore was whether the employees, through their values, felt connected to the goals of the organization. Could they bring their values to work?

Western Financial's success had been built on a deep foundation of trust in the CEO and his leadership team. Rarely have I met employees who believed so strongly in their leadership. They would do anything for these people. In many ways, this trust gave the leadership team a tremendous amount of slack in being able to conduct business in an informal manner. For example, the compensation plan for the sales representatives in the field often did not come out until halfway through the fiscal year. Every year the organization would tweak the commission structure to encourage certain types of policy and discourage others. This meant that sales representatives did not know which types of case or policy would bring in the maximum commission during that year. But the CEO was always upfront about the delays, and as long as the veteran employees trusted their leaders, they were confident that everything would work out okay.

However, this was not so automatic for recently hired employees. They did not share this institutional trust of the leadership team and questioned the sanity of long-term employees willing to work half the year without a compensation plan. A split was growing between the veteran and the newer employees, who did not see themselves as part of the same type of team as the veteran employees did. It was not clear to newer employees how they could connect their own personal values to the company's ambiguously defined goals and whether team players or lone wolves would be more successful in this organization. In interviews with managers and line employees together, I would hear this split in attitudes. Old-timers would laugh about the craziness of the informality of the compensation plan or how all hell would break loose during the fourth quarter. Newer employees would look at them as if they were crazy.

This issue is a common problem for leaders at all levels. As you develop close working relationships with people with whom you enjoy a sense of mutual trust, assuming that all new employees will follow the same pattern is easy. But so is forgetting that those long-standing relationships might have been forged in a different era for the company, perhaps when it was smaller or when reps had more time to be in the field.

Leaders at Western Financial had not developed the means to inculcate trust among newer employees even though these newer people were critical to Western Financial's future, and it had not aligned its organizational goals with individual principles. The organization knew it needed highly motivated, creative, and smart people who could see all of the issues and challenges and put together the right package of offerings for customers. But what could Western's leaders do to keep that kind of employee fully engaged and committed?

Through the values assessment process, we discovered that a strong disincentive for these high-performing employees was a perceived lack of empowerment to do their jobs. The newer employees saw an emerging contradiction that could not be counterbalanced merely by trust in the leadership. The organization said it wanted self-motivated independent thinkers, but employees at all levels saw corporate promulgating more rigid policies that restricted how they were able to do their jobs. In the eyes of employees, the flexibility and discretion they needed to massage a good customer application into closed business was slowly but surely being taken away. As employees began to feel that Western Financial's leadership was more focused on the global organization than on the needs of its representatives in the field, concern increased about each employee's ability to direct his or her own success. The independence that allowed individual employees to achieve financial success had been the recipe for Western's ever improving organizational performance year after year. Now it felt threatened.

It became clear to Western Financial's leadership that they had to find a way to balance their need to meet guidelines from corporate headquarters with the need to give employees and managers more control over their work. Senior leadership decided that each manager needed to determine which kinds of decisions could be delegated down and then support his or her people when they used their new authority to make independent decisions. These two elements—creating an emotional connection for employees and then enabling them to work with a strong sense of autonomy—are the keys to building commitment.

Creating commitment is a process that leaders can replicate through connection and autonomy.

CREATING CONNECTION

Employees are engaged and willing to go beyond their own self-interest if there is alignment between their own core values and the organization's goals and desired values. Do they see themselves in the organization? Do the corporate principles reflect their own?

We know that in most large organizations, employees embody the communal level of awareness. What do these values look like with regard to commitment? In many organizations that I have worked with, the call from the employees is, "We want a sense of belonging." Employees are looking for two things. First, they want their leaders to create a compelling vision to which they can apply their latent sense of loyalty. Second, they want to feel that their sense of commitment is well placed. They want to be sure that they themselves are valued by the organization. In short, they want a mission to belong to and a community to belong to.

Within a large organization, employees can feel connected in a number of ways. We work within concentric circles of people and relationships, each with its own dynamic. There are the people with whom we work most closely, whether by virtue of physical proximity or because we are on the same project. There is our location, then our business unit or division, and then the company itself. Each of these circles poses its own challenges and opportunities for identity and connection. The organization's goal is to replicate the closeness that people feel to their immediate coworkers as a connection to the entire organization.

What is it like at that innermost concentric circle? That is where we show our true communal awareness values. We feel an emotional connection to the people we see all day. We know about each other's families and interests. We can joke and laugh and even share our aggravation at how "corporate" is treating us.

How does an organization extend those feelings to outer circles? Establishing a wider sense of identity or pride will take more than posters in the cafeteria or banners over the front door. Employees need to see how they fit in. They need a clear idea of their role in the grand scheme of things.

The key step is to create clarity among the leadership team as to where you would like to direct employees' sense of loyalty and allegiance. For large organizations with multiple divisions, this can be a complicated challenge. For example, employees may have strong loyalties to the company for which they have worked together, but little loyalty—or sometimes even hostility—for the larger company that has bought them out, all of which may make it hard for the corporate leadership to achieve the synergies it has in mind.

For example, at USZ, the global manufacturing and electronics company introduced in Chapter Two, the concentric circles in which employees felt loyalty and those in which managers would have liked the employees to feel connected were as clearly demarcated as the rings of a tree. USZ owned hundreds of companies in a variety of businesses. One particular business unit where I spent considerable time had several rural manufacturing facilities. Within each facility were multiple buildings, in each of which was produced a particular product or component. And within each building were multiple teams responsible for various aspects of the production process.

At the work group level, people worked very closely together and, in many cases, had done so for years. It was a true work family. People knew each other well, shared personal experiences, and held common values. Since each building housed a specific project, many of these work groups bonded together, acquiring their own sense of coherence. Every employee knew when the program had been successful and the project management was well known throughout the building.

Moving out from the project buildings to the concentric circle of the entire facility, things tended to break down. When I visited the rural Alabama facility, for example, I found little sense of collective identity. The general manager of the facility was seen as a conduit of corporate policy, and the workforce did not respect him. Management's attempts to create a local identity always seemed to fall flat. There was no logical reason that there should be "One Team," as a banner over the front gate proclaimed. This leader never brought the employees together as a single unit. Since each group was working on its own projects, there was little coordination between groups.

A different USZ facility had a much tighter sense of identity. One manager there told me, "As long as employees are in the loop, they are willing to go along." This facility's leadership, knowing that the employees had a strong desire to feel connected and committed, worked hard to satisfy the workforce's need for news and information and being in the loop. In return, there was an openness and a willingness to trust decisions and give the facility leadership the benefit of the doubt. The question for leaders here is whether creating a sense of identity to the physical location of the office or plant is important. If you would benefit from employees having a sense of identity beyond their immediate work group or product group, then affirmative efforts are needed to generate those ties. Employees are not going to make those links on their own.

For many corporations, the next concentric circle beyond the physical location or facility is the business unit. In many cases, business units are artificial entities concocted by leaders to create a certain operational coherence; they really have no meaning to the people who actually work in them. The business unit to which USZ's Alabama facility reported had been created as part of the internal reorganization, and for the vast majority of employees, it was irrelevant to their sense of identity. They had their emotional connection to the people with whom they worked and a sense of pride in being part of the global organization, but no connection at all to the business unit in between.

When I conducted interviews at yet another facility within the same business unit, managers, supervisors, and employees from different buildings and projects reminisced fondly about a recent Tiger team experience. (Tiger teams are ad hoc groups of technical specialists working to solve a specific quality or manufacturing problem.) At this facility, teams from corporate headquarters and other functional departments came to the facility and invited hourly employees, supervisors, and managers into a multiday process to solve a major production problem. The employees loved it. They were involved and able to contribute to the solutions; people listened to them and respected their experience and practical insights. In this way, their business unit meant something important to them. There are opportunities to create identity and connection at the business unit level if leadership seeks it.

The outermost circle was the global corporation itself. Although there was pride in the household-name brand of the company, there was very little connection between most of the local staff and the corporate leadership from the parent organization. If anything, there was resentment. Every time managers from corporate headquarters flew into the rural facility on the corporate jet, they made a point of how far away it was and how long it had taken to get there. They spent most of their time at the facility looking at their BlackBerries and trying to make travel arrangements to return home as soon as possible. But for the employees who lived in that area, the facility was not far away at all. It was their home. The local staff was expected to give these visiting executives their full attention, but it never seemed to be a two-way street. How could the local staff be committed to the organization if their needs and interests in actually making the products never seemed important to those who represented the organization?

Of course, things were not always rosy for those corporate executives either. There was tremendous frustration at the business unit's headquarters. This corporate center housed the engineering, quality, and design teams that coordinated with the various manufacturing facilities within the business unit. The mood was grim. In interviews with individual contributors, such as engineers, I was told: "People do not feel that they are part of a family here. They do not feel that anyone cares about them." It was here that I met the engineer who had reluctantly come to the conclusion that "if you don't ask questions, they won't think you're stupid."

Things were no better at corporate headquarters, where employees coordinated global support functions, such as procurement and contracting, while also supporting matrixed business unit headquarters in other states. It was hard for them to feel connected to the company. Headquarters didn't actually make anything, so they did not feel that they were part of the production teams they supported and felt that they were perceived as not adding value. They felt isolated walking around the quiet halls of the corporate headquarters where people worked on different projects that were themselves in different locations. Unable to live their communal awareness values, these employees fell back on a basic fear of being worthless.

What did this do to productivity? The isolation caused people to work in narrow silos, which inhibited collaboration. These employees wanted to collaborate, but the organizational structure and the way work assignments and rewards were allocated kept people focused on whatever they had to do right now, even if they intuitively knew that broader cooperation and coordination would be better for the company and much more enjoyable for them. Without a strong sense of a common purpose, employees found themselves falling back to protecting their self-interest. They didn't like how that felt, but there didn't seem to be anything they could do about it.

We can learn from their predicament that the key to unlocking collaboration is to make it clear what the corporate objective is and how employees fit into that objective. When these folks sought out others to collaborate, they heard: "My priority isn't your priority" or "Your goals don't matter to me." USZ leadership had not made it clear that although these employees had some goals that were irrelevant to other groups, they also had goals that were shared—which *should* matter to colleagues in other offices and other departments. Without this clarity, latent values of collaboration remain just that—latent— showing up on the surveys as strong personal values and desired culture values but not as actual culture values.

Connection means much more than good corporate communications and serves a far greater purpose than conveying information. Leaders need to determine the highest level of the organization to which every employee needs to be connected and then ensure that managers are making those connections. Of course, each employee needs to have a sense of common purpose with members of his or her team. Does that sense of connection need to extend out to the facility? The business unit? The parent company? For every level at which the connections are essential or useful and not just nice-to-haves, leaders need to develop a plan of action to make and maintain those connections.

One approach is to establish teams that cut across the various levels at which employees need to feel connected. These teams need to have clear missions to accomplish something useful for which the members are accountable. One client of mine took this approach. Leadership understood the importance of keeping employees at various locations connected with the teams that manufactured the products, as well as with the organization as a whole. Teamwork was the guiding organizational principle for allocating work. To avoid confusion and promote accountability, there was a clear point of contact for every step of the production process. Every employee had a specific person with whom to discuss challenges in getting the work done. Individual contributors were invited to share best practices with their peers throughout the organization. Engineers told me that they loved to attend best practices meetings, where they had a chance to learn about other projects in the organization and to see how other groups were handling similar types of problem. These meetings created a tremendous esprit de corps.

In other companies the glue that creates connection for employees is true alignment of the core personal values of the employees and the stated values and principles of the organization. Timberland, for example, successfully capitalizes on the personal values of its workforce. The employee base is a self-selected band of corporate social responsibility zealots. Timberland leaders told me that while their consumers were "light green" in terms of wanting environmentally friendly products (as long as they didn't cost more), their employees were "dark green," that is, deeply committed to Timberland's values of social responsibility and environmental leadership. It becomes clear to Timberland employees that Timberland is not the best place to work for those who do not share those values. Employees are expected to participate in social responsibility programs, above and beyond their demanding workloads; only those for whom these extra activities are compatible with their personal values will find the extra effort satisfying rather than burdensome.

At first blush, alignment of the core personal values of the employees and the stated values and principles of the organization seems to
be how Walmart created a cadre of managers able to conduct themselves so heroically after Hurricane Katrina. More than 75 percent
of Walmart managers are hired from the ranks of hourly employees.
They have been groomed to display an extraordinary loyalty to the
organization, and many genuinely feel that Walmart has given them
an opportunity they would not have been given anywhere else. Part
of Walmart's process to create such loyalty is to force a distinction
between a manager's identification with the store community in which
he or she came up through the ranks and his or her identification
with Walmart as a whole. Perhaps it is for this reason that Walmart
has determined that it is difficult for a store manager to enforce labor
rules and be a tough enough supervisor at the same store at which
he or she was once one of the hourly employees. Walmart therefore
insists that all employees promoted to the manager level must move
to a new store, often hundreds of miles away.[7] For Walmart managers
to succeed, they must embody and feel comfortable with the hierarchical and no-nonsense adherence to the rules that the organization
demands.[8]

In summary, connection is based on the organization's understanding of what motivates its employees (their principles and beliefs) and
then taking steps to show that the organization welcomes and supports
those values. For some organizations and some employees, that connection can be made by permitting the employees to achieve goals that
satisfy values at the performance level of awareness. But for most
employees, you need to nurture their desire to feel like valued members
of the organization at the communal level of awareness.

GRANTING AUTONOMY

While aligning principles and beliefs with organizational goals is critical to creating the sense of belonging that employees seek, building

commitment also requires that each individual employee have an opportunity to feel personally fulfilled in his or her work. A considerable research literature exists on what fulfills us at work; here I integrate some of that work, with a focus on what will make your people feel committed to your organization, able to live their core values while doing their work.

Most employees would like to do their jobs as well as they can. When the organization creates opportunities (linked to its business goals) for employees to grow and feel fulfilled (satisfying key personal values), employees feel a stronger sense of commitment. For example, leadership frequently determines that the organization cannot achieve its goals unless its employees have certain values, such as personal responsibility, and certain skills, such as flexibility and adaptability, that call for initiative and problem solving. Leaders must then take care to keep the employees who have such values and skills motivated and engaged. This in turn calls for a work environment that encourages initiative and problem solving rather than stifling them.

Personal autonomy—the employees' and managers' sense that they have ownership of some aspect of their work—is essential to creating commitment. Managers who otherwise feel an emotional connection to their company may not be able to sustain their commitment if they cannot work with a sense of personal responsibility and autonomy. It is true that for some people, their commitment to an organization is so great that they will take on any task just to be a part of the whole, but they are exceptional. Most of us need to feel that we have some control over our jobs in order to sustain our engagement and commitment. Yet we also accept that we cannot simply do whatever we want. This balancing act between having control and being controlled is at the heart of our sense of commitment to the organization.

The challenges of granting personal autonomy can be seen more clearly in terms of the levels of awareness. As leaders come to understand where their people are operating from and where they wish or need to be, they can see what it is their people need to have some control over.

Level 1: Survival Awareness

Let's first look at the survival level of awareness. This is where we see the most basic need to have control and for employees to feel controlled. For many leaders, especially those who supervise hourly employees, it is hard to imagine how to grant more autonomy without losing control. So I ask those leaders: What is behind the need for control? Is it really the case that your employees won't produce unless you are on top of them? Or is that belief a vestige from the past?

I recently worked with a manufacturing organization that had two facilities. Employees at one were engaged and felt that they were able to contribute to the organization. They had pride and a sense of proprietary concern that the company stay on track to meet its goals. At the other facility, tensions ran high, turnover was a major challenge, and leaders felt they couldn't let employees out of their sight.

Autonomy accounted for much of the difference. Hourly employees at the high-performing facility told me that they received their instructions from their supervisor in the morning and then were left to do their work, knowing that the supervisors, as well as support functions such as engineering and quality, were available if they needed help. The supervisors told me that there was no reason to be heavy-handed with the workers since they knew how to do their jobs.

Supervisors at the other facility did not trust the hourly workers to meet the production requirements without active supervision. Production deadlines were tight, and the supervisors were under pressure. When I spoke to these hourly employees, they expressed a persistent sense of vulnerability. When supervisors came down to the floor with a change in the production schedule, they would hover over the operators to make sure the transition to new parts was made quickly. Operators did not feel they could talk with their supervisors about where they were in the process and the best way to meet the changed goals. So they switched gears and did the best they could. But they felt no sense of commitment to the organization because they could not take any pride in their work or even any sense of ownership over their part in the production process.

In the end, one of the most effective ways to keep tough goals aligned with values is to give each individual employee and manager as much latitude and discretion as possible to work to the best of his or her ability. People can arrive at their own alignment of values and goals if they are given the space to do so.

Level 2: Relationship Awareness

In many organizations, senior leaders are eager to increase their employees' sense of personal autonomy. Many leaders I have worked with relish the fact that employees can work independently and can be responsible for getting their work done. The problem is often the lower ranks of management. What senior leaders want is not always what frontline supervisors and middle managers deliver. In these situations, leaders are grappling with challenges to autonomy at the relationship level of awareness.

In an aircraft manufacturing company I worked with, operators on the plant floor lamented leadership's increasing micromanagement. With growing pressure to meet ever increasing production quotas with reduced staff came tempers that were short as deadlines approached. Lost in the conversation was an acknowledgment that the veteran workers knew how to get the job done if they were only given the chance to do so. Sometimes this is called tribal knowledge: veteran employees who have seen it all have developed ways to get things done. They know how the system works and what has to happen for deadlines to be met. In many organizations, however, corporate leaders show little respect for this informal knowledge base, convinced that clear processes are all that is needed and that tribal practices need to be tamed. (To be fair, the tribal practices may actually pose performance or ethical risks, particularly if the work of the tribe is being integrated into a larger context than the one in which it first emerged.)

There was often friction in this plant between the manufacturing engineers responsible for adherence to production specifications and the operators who actually produced the components. When the relationship was not working well, it resulted in inefficiency, a tremendous diversion of energy into solving interpersonal problems, and—worst of all—defective parts going out the door, with the resulting returns and rework.

For example, in many manufacturing processes, engineers develop a "tolerance stack" for the various components of the final product. Each element in the complete product has its own set of tolerances in terms of minimum and maximum variances that may be permitted, such as how closely pieces must fit together. It can happen, however, that multiple parts, when stacked together, are each within specifications but as a group are inoperable. During one shift, an operator turned to the manufacturing engineer and said, "I can't put a bolt through this piece because the holes are not lining up properly. What do I do?" The manufacturing engineer, consulting his documents, replied, "I don't see a problem. The specifications are fine. The bolt should go in just fine." The operator, who had to build a part, not a specification, looked at the engineer as if he were an idiot. The entire paradigm for the relationship between the operator and the engineer was wrong. The lack of mutual personal respect for the skills and ability of the other made it impossible to discuss a problem without the exchange becoming personal and destructive. Mutual respect in this case goes deeper than being nice to one another. It affects how employees see their self-worth and their perceived worth to the company.

An example of a successful best practice to respond to this challenge was found elsewhere in the same plant, where there was a different relationship between another manufacturing engineer, Jim, and the operators. Jim was a veteran engineer, and the operators loved him. He was tough and held them to tough standards, but he was fair. When operators ran into problems, Jim's first response was, "Let's see what the problem is. What can we do to solve it?" Something as simple as having the operator and the engineer solve the problem together could relieve the tensions, as well as provide invaluable learning opportunities for the younger operators. Jim would offer some suggestions and then let the operators take ownership of that issue so they could discover the right course of action themselves. These operators gained a sense of autonomy by being treated as respected members of the team.

Level 3: Performance Awareness

The solutions to granting more personal autonomy are often not as simple as basic respect. Many times, granting more autonomy means someone higher up must delegate authority that they may not want to give away. Sometimes it stems from ego issues. Other times it is a function of how the organization has established its work processes. In many instances, established processes have never been evaluated in terms of how they bear on the performance level of awareness.

For example, at Western Financial, employees hungered for greater autonomy and empowerment. The company wanted sales representatives and underwriters to work together as a team. When there is close coordination between the sales reps and the underwriter, cases can be approved more quickly and the organization has a chance to offer the best pricing with the lowest risk. However, that was not always how it worked out.

Because the sales representatives were commission based, they felt the most pressure to have every case approved, and as quickly as possible. The underwriters were willing to be team players, but each underwriter had specific guidelines for approving any particular case. In fact, those guidelines were so strict that few applications could qualify. Therefore, the underwriter almost always had to get authority from his or her manager to approve the case as the sales representatives impatiently tapped their toes. When the underwriter could not get instant approval on a particular application (because his or her manager wasn't around), the sales representative would turn to his or her sales manager, who was often able to get access to the underwriter's manager even before the underwriter could. The underwriting manager, without consulting with the underwriter, would hear the situation from the sales manager and approve the application. So the sales representative got what he or she was looking for, and the underwriter felt undermined. He or she could have made the same call as the manager but was hamstrung by the guidelines. The underwriters felt that they lost face with the sales reps and were not considered a critical part of the overall sales team. Whatever positive things this process may have accomplished, it lowered morale and created a lot of frustration.

Senior leaders had never focused on this lack of autonomy as being a source of frustration in the organization. As they saw it, escalating cases so that sales managers had to coordinate with underwriting managers was just the way they did business. However, once leaders made the connection between a poor process and employee frustration and disengagement, the matter took on a greater sense of urgency. Sales representatives, sales managers, and underwriting managers began to include the underwriters in the review process. Once everyone acknowledged that the problem was not underwriters' intransigence but an effort to have checks and balances in underwriting approvals, the individual underwriters could be seen as part of the solution to the problem rather than the cause. Procedures were set up to make it easier for underwriters to flag sales representatives' issues and forward them up within the underwriting organization. Underwriting managers were able to make appropriate variances with the coordination of the underwriters, reducing the need for the sales professionals to escalate every request. The underwriters felt that they were core members of the team because they were now able to initiate the problem-solving process.

LOCKING IN COMMITMENT

How can a company ensure that it is building effective commitment that covers both sides of the equation, creating a sense of connection and encouraging personal autonomy? From my experience working with organizations seeking to create cultures of commitment, several key building blocks must be in place, working up through the levels of awareness.

Leaders must first ensure that there are no challenges at the survival level of awareness. Leadership must be able to convey to the workforce that success and profit are not goals in themselves, but will come as a result of meeting other goals. In other words, leaders of successful companies with healthy cultures don't have to drill the need for profit into their employees' heads. Everyone knows that the organization must be profitable. Leaders successful at building commitment know that profits will come if their employees are able to bring their power values of integrity, commitment, and transparency to work. Otherwise the organization is driven by fear, which can sometimes produce "results" but not sustainable commitment. Leadership must be able to create a broader vision of success, which can ignite employees' passion or at least their dedication. Employees must be able to see a connection between what is important to them and what is important to the organization.

The key here is control. Ask yourself and your colleagues to identify where you think employees in the organization feel that they are either in control or being controlled. If you don't have a sense of how they feel, it may be time to ask. (In Chapter Seven, I detail specific steps you can take to assess your culture.) Are the areas where employees feel controlled legitimate and justified? If so, then communicate the reasons to your people. If it is done in a respectful manner, they will understand, and it will become a nonissue.

At the relationship level of awareness, leadership must ensure that employees feel respected and appreciated. The theme that emerges from organizations where employees have a sense of commitment is that they feel listened to. In any organization, employees at all levels are very attuned to whether leadership hears what they say. They do not expect their leaders to implement every request or suggestion, but they do expect their input to be sought out and valued. When I see "listening" among an organization's current culture values, I know that I am likely to find a fully engaged and committed workforce.

Of course, commitment can be challenged at the performance level of awareness if employees feel that their managers do listen but nothing seems to change. Commitment requires action. It is much better to fully implement a small plan than to make big promises and underperform. For example, the sincere desire to engage employees often begins well with a formal engagement survey or an informal request from an employee or a team, but ends once the input has been collected. One manager told me that she appreciated her company's efforts to be responsive to employees' needs, but, she added, "For two years the company has been asking me how I feel, and now I want to see them actually do something with all this data."

In most of the values assessments I have undertaken, I have found that while employees embody more personal values at the communal level of awareness than at any other level, they wish their organization's culture embodied more values at the engagement level of awareness than at any other. They want to use their values at the communal level of awareness, including the 3 power values, to create a flexible organization marked by teamwork, adaptability, and even the ability to continuously improve processes. These are the attributes that support true engagement. A clear program that embodies the attributes of the engagement level of awareness, outlined in Chapter Three, will keep employees deeply committed to the organization.

When employees feel secure at these four foundational levels of awareness, they will feel more open to applying their natural desire to commit themselves to the organization and its goals. I recently came back to a global organization to conduct a follow-on values assessment. Two years earlier, this business had been reorganized, and local managers were having trouble balancing their obligations to manage the business with the need to please their corporate bosses. People were stressed and frustrations high. Employees complained about inconsistency and confusion dominating the current culture. But now things were running smoothly. What had changed? From hourly operators to supervisors to local leadership, I heard the same answer: corporate headquarters was letting them take ownership of their own business. They were acting autonomously. Sure, they had aggressive goals they had to meet. But corporate leadership was conscious of not imposing uniform decision making across the entire enterprise if it would interfere with the need to develop tight teams within each division. The team with the largest concentric circle that could create a sense of commitment—that is, the business unit—was given responsibility for meeting corporate objectives and the autonomy to determine *how* to meet them.

Leaders led. The business unit leaders did not hide behind broader corporate policies to justify tough actions or unpleasant changes. They engaged their staffs at all levels to participate in developing the best means to implement strategies to meet their objectives. Leaders were not out looking for people to blame if deadlines were being missed. They were asking employees how they could help. A sense of connection and personal responsibility was driving commitment for this company.

Organizations need to cover both sides of the values and goals equation to garner commitment. The organization wants its employees to feel that they can live their personal values at work, knowing that if they can, they will be more passionate, dedicated, and connected. Employees need to feel that they have some control over their work flow or decisions. Personal autonomy generates engagement. But sustained commitment happens only when employees can claim both a sense of connection and a sense of personal autonomy.

Transparency Aligns
Principles and Standards

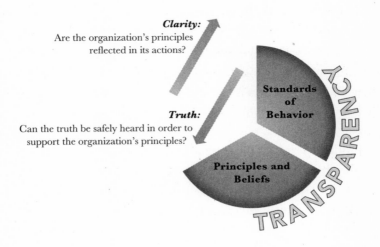

J eff Swartz was pissed off. On one morning in June 2009, the CEO of the Timberland Company had received more than sixty-five thousand e-mails from Greenpeace supporters expressing concern that the leather in Timberland's products might be sourced from cattle grazing on pastures created from illegally cleared Amazon rain forests.

None of Timberland's senior leadership wanted to make time for this issue at a time that the company was struggling to stay profitable in the midst of the recession. Trusting in their environmental credentials, they thought the right strategy would be to end this potentially volatile public relations issue as quickly as possible. Since Timberland did not purchase a significant percentage of its leather from the Amazon region anyway, it would be easy to publicly announce that the company would just not buy leather from disputed regions.

Swartz couldn't settle for that. Confident in his company's commitment to social responsibility, he was put off by the aggressive, scattershot style of Greenpeace's campaign. He wanted to do the right thing but wasn't sure yet what that was. As he began asking questions, he discovered that Timberland did not know where most of the leather it sourced in Brazil actually came from. In fact, neither Greenpeace nor anyone in the apparel business had ever traced the supply chain there beyond the tanneries to the actual ranches where the cattle were raised.

So Swartz decided to tackle the issue head-on. He and his company were willing to admit what they didn't know and were confident enough in their ability to live their values to pursue an inquiry in the public eye without knowing where it would end up. Timberland began to study where its leather was sourced and how the company could influence producers to do the right thing. Greenpeace later praised Timberland for taking a leadership role in getting to the heart of the issue. As Swartz said, "In times of tension, watch and listen. That's when you learn just how committed you are to your principles—and how committed your team and your partners and even your competitors are to theirs."[1]

WHY TRANSPARENCY MATTERS

Chapter Five looked at control as it relates to encouraging or discouraging an individual employee's sense of commitment. In many ways, transparency plays a similar role in today's interconnected world. Leaders cannot be aware of every issue that affects their company and cannot be involved in every decision. Maintaining tight control over information flows no longer works in a connected world in which employees and consumers demand access to information 24/7. Transparency therefore plays a critical role in managing a culture made up of people you don't see every day—or ever. In many ways, transparency is the pinnacle of the process of aligning culture in order to remove the roadblocks to performance. It helps employees manage the most difficult of their human behavior foibles—such as self-deception, rationalization, and disengagement—so that they can fully live their values at work.

Transparency Defined

Transparency is a term that lends itself to many definitions. Three definitions are commonly used in business:

1. Lack of hidden agendas and conditions, accompanied by the availability of full information required for collaboration, cooperation, and collective decision-making.
2. Minimum degree of disclosure to which agreements, … transactions and business practices are open to all for verification.
3. Essential condition for a free and open exchange whereby the rules and reasons behind regulatory measures are fair and clear to all participants.[2]

In financial reporting, transparency helps investors and creditors better evaluate an organization's financial condition. Stakeholders expect clear, reliable, consistent, and transparent reporting of events. In addition to helping investors make better decisions, transparency can also increase overall confidence in the fairness of the markets themselves. Since the 2002 passage of the Sarbanes-Oxley legislation in the United States, transparency has been a cornerstone of efforts to improve corporate governance. It enables a board of directors to evaluate management's effectiveness and to take early corrective action. If the information in financial reports is transparent, investors and others who use that information are less likely to be surprised by undisclosed transactions or events.

Consumers are also demanding that companies provide more accountability and transparency in the area of social and environmental responsibility. Consumers want to know more about the products and services they buy, as there has been a growing trend of consumers' buying brands that align with their own personal interests and beliefs.[3]

None of these definitions fully explains why transparency is so important today. In many ways, it is at the heart of what generates trust. It is the final step in permitting an employee to lower his or her guard and become an actively engaged citizen of the community your organization is trying to create. We all know that no person or company is perfect; to trust people and companies, we need to be able to assess what they are made of and what they stand for. We therefore need them to be open—willing to share their strengths and weaknesses. This is the heart of transparency.

Transparency Is Expected

Ten or fifteen years ago, leaders may have had a choice of whether to be more open in their communications and business dealings. But today leaders no longer have a choice whether to embrace transparency. That train has left the station. The advent of social networks and 24/7 information has firmly placed corporations in the middle of the information highway. It is very difficult for any organization to conceal information about itself or its employees in this digital age. That does not mean, however, that fully embracing open information is easy.

Younger employees who have grown up in an age of instant and continuous information have very different approaches to communication, privacy, and transparency than do older managers and leaders. The younger employees almost intuitively understand that transparency is the only way to get access to the specific information they need, and they are comfortable with perpetual collaboration on social networks. They expect to be able to communicate with whomever they wish whenever they want. This has created drastically different expectations of collaboration and teamwork for employees who need access to multiple people all the time. If organizations do not adjust their policies and attitudes to these new ways of doing business, the foundations of commitment discussed in Chapter Five—connection and responsibility—will be seriously at risk.

Transparency Keeps Information Flowing

A transparent approach is essential for effective operations in large organizations in which every employee must communicate and coordinate freely with multiple layers in a complex matrix. In some ways, it's a matter of simple math. In the old days, a leader in a hierarchical organization had control not only over the people who reported to him but also over the flow of information up to his bosses. In today's matrixed organizations, with dotted-line responsibilities linking people to dozens of coworkers throughout the organization, such control is much more tenuous, and in any case, the free flow of information is vital. There isn't enough time in the day to negotiate with everyone who has information you need. It has to be made available, and it has to be reliable. When I recently asked employees at a global retail giant why honesty was so important to them as a personal value, the response was the same from all quarters of the organization: "We are running too fast for me not to be able to rely on the data being provided by someone else in the organization." Transparency was the currency that kept the company going.

Transparency is also vital in mitigating several of the leading indicators of misconduct. When leaders assert that their people should always "do the right thing," is it always clear what that means? If the line between right and wrong for a given issue were clear, then only someone intentionally engaging in misconduct would cross it. But the line is rarely clear in a complex situation that pits competing principles, goals, and standards against each other.

As a leader, you can never know what your organization's specific goals and standards will be down the road—that is, what decisions will have to be made—so you need to focus on how decisions are made. Organizations need to develop clarity as to how they want their employees and managers to approach tough issues, ask tough questions, and thoughtfully discuss the best course of action. It is therefore no surprise that, according to the Corporate Executive Board, a culture of retaliation, in which employees are uncomfortable raising concerns, is a leading indicator of misconduct.[4]

Transparency Aligns Principles and Standards

While the necessity of a culture of transparency is clear (pun intended), it is not so obvious how to achieve it. Transparency is not a value or a cultural attribute that leadership can impose at will. A powerful endorsement from the CEO will not do the trick. So how do you create a culture based on transparency? What are the specific steps to create an organization that engenders trust among its customers and employees? You need to translate the worthy concept of transparency into specific behaviors that you can manage.

Transparency is the end result of a focused and well-defined process that builds toward it. The companies that have successfully instilled transparency have systematically assessed what factors thwart being open and then have developed systems to ensure that the blocking behaviors are nullified and the positive behaviors encouraged.

The journey to transparency begins by defining the building blocks that create it so that we can identify the kinds of behavior the organization will need to inculcate.

What does it mean to be more open? Whether you are evaluating an individual or an organization, you can observe what they are doing and get a sense of what they stand for. You need to see both. You may initially believe that an organization shares your principles and beliefs, but your sense of identification with it will decline if you observe that its actions belie those principles. For example, you may see a manager asking for input and inviting contributions, but if you subsequently observe that the organization's principles favor internal competition rather than collaboration—perhaps even that the information you share could be used against you—you certainly will not fully engage.

Transparency connects and aligns what an organization does—its standards of behavior—with what it stands for—its principles and beliefs. When that happens, the organization is characterized by both clarity—everyone knows what is behind the leaders' actions and decisions—and truth—anyone can safely ask questions and point out gaps between actions and values. The ability of employees and leadership to openly discuss the conflicts between principles and standards is at the heart of transparency.

As you are about to read, the process by which Timberland's management team grappled with the leather-sourcing issue highlights the challenges that even a socially aware organization must overcome to maintain a high degree of transparency. Timberland is all about values. Its mission is "to equip people to make a difference in their world. We do this by creating outstanding products and by trying to make a difference in the communities where we live and work." But Timberland is also a retailer in a highly competitive market.[5] The challenge is to identify how new situations affect the company's values and which standards of behavior will be used to address those situations while remaining consistent with those values. Although no company is perfect, the candor by which Timberland approaches its challenges has much to teach about how to use transparency as a tool to create a dynamic culture.

As we saw with the other power values, there are nuances in how transparency aligns a pair of cultural building blocks—in this case, principles and standards—depending on which we take as our vantage point.

CLARITY

How well are the organization's principles aligned with its standards of behavior? Once we know the organization's principles, we have to ask how well leaders have defined standards of behavior that support those principles. Every employee must be able to answer the same question: Can I align my principles with the organization's standards of behavior? To know this, every employee must have a sense of how the organization makes its decisions, implements its policies, and goes about its day-to-day business. This discussion of the power value of integrity incorporated the need for consistency in how employees and managers do their work. Here we explore the decision-making process. Do employees and managers understand it? Are decisions in your organization made in secret, or is there an openness to the process that invites participation? Chapter Five showed how serious an issue this can be: sales representatives at Western Financial could never be sure whether a prospective case would be accepted or rejected, and their maneuvering around this uncertainty created risk for the company.

What are your organization's priorities? Which principles are being weighed in any major decision, and how is that process conducted? There must be clarity as to what your organization stands for so that each employee can predict the process by which a particular decision will be resolved. For each principle, there must be defined behaviors or a clear process by which a standard will be defined when it is needed. Of course, these behaviors and standards must be consistent with the principles they are meant to support, a requirement that sounds obvious but is not always so easy to fulfill. The more clarity there is about the behaviors and processes that support an organization's principles, the more transparent the organization.

An example shows how such clarity can help an organization make tough decisions. A frequent challenge for Timberland arises when the company feels that it is acting in accordance with its principles but certain external stakeholders disagree. In 2011, for example, Timberland hired both union and nonunion labor to build out a new store in New York City. When the local unions protested Timberland's inclusion of nonunion workers, the company had to decide whether it would yield to the pressure. Because Timberland had already devised its own explicit criteria for fair labor practices in terms of wages and conditions—that is, the standards that would support its core value of corporate citizenship—it felt confident that it could meet those criteria in this instance without having to hire only union workers. Timberland engaged the union leadership, the union made adjustments, and the project continued. According to Robin Giampa, Timberland's director of communications, "If everyone is clear on the values, it is easier to make tough decisions."[6] For Giampa, having a clear sense of what the company stood for permitted her to respond more quickly and more authoritatively. In many organizations, any decision that has an impact on external stakeholders and could be picked up in the press involves management in a crisis response, creating tremendous distractions. Permitting managers to act according to your organization's principles is, if nothing else, an efficiency and productivity tool because it saves everyone a deal of trouble.

Betsy Blaisdell, Timberland's senior manager of environmental stewardship, offered additional insight on how transparency can make decisions easier. Greenpeace's protest over Timberland's use of Brazilian leather did require a full leadership response, but clarity shortened the decision-making process. Despite Timberland's leadership role in corporate responsibility, top executives never forget that they are running a public company with a primary obligation to its shareholders. They therefore need to decide which issues require intervention and which do not. According to Betsy, there are three determining factors:

1. *Is the issue material to Timberland's core business?* Because leather and rubber constitute more than 80 percent of its supply chain, Timberland felt obligated to fully understand the sourcing issues for those materials.
2. *Will the solution to the problem affect other issues Timberland faces?* It was easy for the team to decide that getting to the heart of the Amazon leather supply chain would help the company evaluate other supply chain issues.

3. *Would Timberland be acting alone, or would the intervention be collaborative?* Even as a strong advocate of corporate responsibility, Timberland does not have the size, depth, and resources to be at the leading edge of every issue. In this case, Timberland asked the Leather Working Group, a multistakeholder association that develops and maintains a protocol to assess the compliance and environmental performance of tanners in the leather industry, to take the lead in investigating the sourcing issue.[7]

Timberland had developed clear guidelines for its leaders to use in deciding what issues it needs to engage in and which it can safely bypass. Understanding the relationship between their principles and their standards of behavior helps the leadership team decide which social issues are directly connected to their core business and are therefore bottom-line issues. Timberland does not feel obliged to prove anything or create a public relations victory by insisting that its suppliers meet the highest possible level. Organizational survival and profitability are values too, for Timberland and for its suppliers. Cost therefore should not be excluded as a factor in living one's values, so long as the values are clear.

For example, Timberland has been trying for years to reduce the levels of hazardous substances in its products; such substances include PVC and solvent adhesives that give off volatile organic compounds (VOCs). This gets to the heart of the trade-off between being environmentally responsible (VOCs are toxic and nasty) and producing quality products (PVC improves the quality of rubber). Timberland does not ignore the fact that it touts environmental responsibility while still using a toxic chemical in its products. Finding alternatives to PVC and solvent adhesives that give off VOCs is costly, especially during recessionary periods. Therefore, Timberland decided not to try to remove all the PVC from its products by a particular date, but rather to commit itself to continually reducing the amounts as best it could.

How well does your organization do in making tough choices that may leave no one happy? What if the best your organization can do today falls short of its long-term objectives? In many organizations, a "failure is not an option" mentality prevents managers and leaders from making realistic decisions that can help employees better understand how to do their work. Instead, employees are handed unrealistic goals and objectives that require fudging budgets and production schedules from the start.

Clarity offers a different option. Instead of overpromising and underdelivering, put the challenge out there and be open and honest about where your company is and what steps it is taking to meet the goal.

For Timberland, profits have to be balanced with principles; neither can be allowed to overwhelm the other. In order to hold itself accountable for reducing the levels of PVC in its products, Timberland decided to include a "nutrition label" of environmental information on its packaging, an idea Swartz got from looking at the nutritional label on a box of breakfast cereal. Timberland's stated commitment was to be accountable for everything it did that affected its environmental footprint, from production to shipping to how the products were sold. The best way to hold people throughout the company accountable (and keep them living their own values) is to communicate openly about how well or poorly the company is meeting those objectives. Stating the percentage of PVC and other hazardous substances right on the label, for all the world to see, forces Timberland's design and production teams to be more accountable and to keep trying to reduce that number in product development. Of course, such transparency also lets external stakeholders see how Timberland is prioritizing its environmental impact.

CAN THE TRUTH BE TOLD?

Organizations that permit clarity in stating how well they are moving toward meeting their goals will go far in having the backing and loyalty of appreciative employees. But clarity requires a culture in which the truth can be heard. What does your organization do when an issue is so hot that you don't even know which standards of behavior to apply? Organizations that can develop ways to manage the unknowns and the tough issues are the ones that have enviable cultures in which employees are fully engaged in taking personal risks for the good of the organization.

The way in which Timberland's leaders addressed the unknowns in the leather-sourcing issue offers insights into the steps any organization can take to instill transparency. Timberland has been able to balance profit with social responsibility in part because it has institutionalized truth seeking. For Jeff Swartz, whenever the company faces a new issue for which there are no clear answers, the only real course of action is to find out what is really going on. Jeff stated in his blog during the Greenpeace incident:

> Given that we don't have "traceability" in the value chain back to the cow grazing in the field, it would have been infinitely easier, when Greenpeace first brought the issue to our mailbox, to simply stop doing business with our Brazilian supplier. No more leather from Brazil, no more issues with tracing hides which may have come from cows grazing in deforested areas of the Amazon rainforest. We're only talking about 7% of our production—so cut and run, right?
>
> Tempting, but not the right thing to do. Disengaging would have solved OUR problem—no more headaches or emails from angry activists—but would do nothing to solve the problem of deforestation. Even as we fumed at the way Greenpeace had approached this issue we asked ourselves, what is the responsible thing to do? Do we walk away and let the beef processors sort this out with Greenpeace, or do we risk further ire, by staying in the conversation and engaging the leather tanner and the beef processor to solve the real environmental challenge? What would you choose to do?[8]

Jerry Erwin, a seventeen-year veteran Timberland senior director who managed the supply chain and was intimately involved in the leather-sourcing issue, said that Timberland would never have thought about the connection between deforestation and its leather supply before Greenpeace raised the issue.[9] Protecting rain forests had been a well-known environmental issue, of course, but it had not been seen as a supply chain issue before. The natural question among Timberland managers was, "How far back up the supply chain do we have to go to determine the environmental and ethical content of the product?"

When is enough enough? This has always been the critical inflection point for organizations struggling to determine which standards are sufficient. Can an organization take comfort in staying within legal or industry guidelines? When does that shelter provide false protection? Sometimes an organization's own reputation can provide a false sense of security. In 2010, Toyota faced a public relations nightmare due to faulty accelerator pedals in several of its models. As long as Toyota was within industry standards, did its reputation for perfectionism oblige it to go beyond them? What did its stakeholders expect? Instead of trying to find a specific point on the spectrum—"*This* is how good we will be"—Timberland has taken the approach of being open about the issue and then showing its commitment to making progress—"This is how good we will *keep trying* to be." Sincere forward momentum can often reduce the need to find a precise balancing point between competing values.

For Timberland, the sourcing of its American leather—88 percent of its leather supply—had never been a problem. Timberland had always relied on U.S. Department of Agriculture (USDA) standards. Through the USDA, Timberland could determine the quality and the environmental and ethical status of its American leather and even trace that leather back to a specific farm if necessary. Brazil was a different matter. Timberland used a Brazilian tannery to supply a Brazilian factory with leather that was used to make inner components of its footwear—items such as collars and lining—which could be made from lighter-weight Brazilian leather. No one had ever done traceability studies of the particular cattle that were the source of this leather, and there was no way to achieve consistent standards in Brazil because each local government imposed its own standards.

When the Timberland team met to address this issue, it seemed too hard to solve because of the many unknowns. And since Brazilian leather was a relatively small percentage of Timberland's total leather product line, some of Timberland's leaders did want to cut and run. However, that would go against Timberland principles that concern the way it conducts its business. Because Timberland strives to make a difference in the communities it serves, it responds to activists, hears them out, and understands the scope of the problem. But it cannot respond to every inquiry. Every leader of such a company must balance the core value of environmental leadership with the need to get one's own job done and the need to keep the company profitable. Timberland's values (with Swartz's urging) helped bring the conversation back to the need to first understand the scope of the problem. Engaging in a traceability exercise would help them understand the scope of this issue in their supply chain and whether there were deeper issues that needed to be resolved.

How does Timberland assure its employees that these kinds of conversations can take place? In what circumstances do people feel uncomfortable raising a red flag? How does an organization create standards for truth seeking?

Timberland, like every other company, has groups competing for their own interests and thus creating values conflicts, such as quality versus profit or production versus work/life balance. For Timberland, there is a healthy conflict in the development and production process. For example, a product could be tagged by the marketing team as a "key marketing style" for the upcoming season, but it may turn out not to be green enough to satisfy the internal environmental watchdogs. One of the challenges in values-driven manufacturing is matching aspirations for environmental leadership with the ability to incorporate higher fashion and quality standards into the product. In the course of designing, developing, and manufacturing a product, it may be determined that some component or aspect of the product does not satisfy Timberland's environmental criteria. Sometimes the company just cannot meet its own combination of standards.

To address these competing interests, Timberland established the fifteen-person interdepartmental Green Working Group. Timberland institutionalizes transparency by stating quite openly the environmental goals it is aspiring to achieve and where it stands currently, even if it is falling short of its own standards. This also helps establish a realistic time frame by which Timberland will seek to meet its stated objectives.

Much of this conversation happens within the Green Working Group. What makes the team successful is the honest conversation among the stakeholders. No one holds back, but courtesy is required. According to Jerry Erwin, each member can call out any statement that is deemed inappropriate, self-serving, or not in furtherance of a common goal. Each member has permission to seek clarity on whether another member's position is intended to meet a group goal or an organizational goal. Also, Timberland is a learning culture in which people can make mistakes so long as they are open and there is a learning process so that the mistakes are not repeated. Each member's freedom to contribute his or her voice to the conversation makes it possible for the Green Working Group to balance Timberland's environmental and production objectives and reach a satisfactory equilibrium.

BUILDING BLOCKS OF TRANSPARENCY

An organization cannot become transparent overnight. It must make its way through incremental steps to create both the necessary trust and processes. To have a culture in which employees know that their decisions will be supported and that questions can be raised, leadership needs to ensure that four essential elements are in place. It must:

- Aggressively enforce its principles and not only its standards. Standards tend to be easier to enforce than principles because standards are more like rules.
- Create a safe place for questions to be raised.
- Ensure that leaders don't become isolated, losing touch with the issues and challenges their employees face. My number one piece of advice on this point to the leaders in my client companies is: Get out from behind your desks!
- Get to the heart of the issue. There are always reasons that people do what they do. If you don't get to the root cause of why the truth cannot be told, then the truth will never be told.

Let's look in detail at each of these elements.

Enforce the Principles

To create transparency, which is built on clarity and truth, your organization must first be clear about its principles—what it stands for—and its standards—what behavior is expected. Then it must enforce those principles and not just the standards.

This isn't as glib as it might seem. Organizations can make the mistake of energetically enforcing their standards while assuming (perhaps not consciously) that this will take care of the principles. If no one is breaking our rules, how can our principles be at risk? But it can happen. Timberland had to face down a temptation to hide behind standards rather than fully live up to its principles. As of 2011, Timberland owned only one factory. Most of its products were produced by suppliers and were the work of approximately 247,000 workers in roughly three hundred factories in thirty-eight countries. These workers are not Timberland employees. Since all apparel companies doing business in developing countries have developed codes of conduct for their contractors, Timberland could safely follow industry guidelines on fair labor practices and have been within the law. But it would not have been enforcing its principles.

Being a values-driven organization, Timberland developed its own standards to allow it to live its values. In 2005, the company shifted away from generating lists of violations for factory owners to resolve (which were then checked to verify improvements). Instead, it chose to work more closely with factory managements to solve the root causes of problems in their factories:

> Whether we are focusing on our own factory or on our third-party contract manufacturers, we work to ensure that all factories comply with our Code of Conduct. But we also seek to do more. We define Earthkeeping as our mission to put commerce and justice at the center of our business platform. In the spirit of Earthkeeping, we believe it is important to go beyond factory walls by protecting the environment in which we operate and the individual workers who produce our products.[10]

Timberland has a unique philosophy of dealing with suppliers. If a business unit manager wishes to work with a supplier that has a record of unsatisfactory work conditions, Timberland will not automatically walk away. Rather, it will ascertain whether the supplier's leadership is serious about improving work conditions in order to be a more reliable partner in the apparel industry. If it is, Timberland will try to create a partnership with the factory rather than function as the compliance police. It will seek to understand the supplier's culture and management and then make a commitment to help the supplier fix issues such as turnover and labor conditions. For the supplier, this helps it position itself to be a trusted partner of other apparel companies worldwide. Timberland enters that supplier's data into the Fair Factories Clearinghouse, a database that any apparel manufacturer can check. Timberland began this type of assessment in 2005, and as of today, it is the only apparel manufacturer conducting itself this way with all of its suppliers. So far, it has assessed over three hundred factories, including those in the United States.

Timberland is interested in seeing its suppliers engage in sustainable change rather than "check the box" compliance. Engaging a supplier's employees is the key. For example, Timberland asks its suppliers to create worker committees to implement the solutions that the supplier and its employees develop to meet Timberland's standards. According to Colleen von Haden, who manages the company's code-of-conduct program with its suppliers,

> By engaging workers directly in our factory assessment process, we believe it is possible to establish trust and a two-way dialogue that ensures factory workers' voices are heard. We've helped train workers and cultivated support from factory management so workers can establish their own Code of Conduct Committees. This enables them to participate in the process of identifying improvement areas and to take part in initiatives to achieve positive change. We've also encouraged factory owners and workers to establish and promote home-grown training programs that encourage workers to share ideas and implement improvements. And we've learned that seeking input from community members—local NGOs, government, industry organizations, other area factories, and other brands that source from the same factories—is integral to ensuring sustainable improvements.[11]

Timberland's assessors become a regular part of the ongoing relationship with that supplier. Each assessor has twenty-five factories in his or her territory and makes periodic visits to see if there are questions and to ensure that the standards are being met. However, it is not up to the assessors alone. Each business unit is also required to ensure that the action plan to which a supplier has committed is being implemented. In fact, a supplier must deliver an action plan derived during the assessment before Timberland can place any orders with that plant.

Will Timberland stop working with a supplier that violates any of the standards to which it has agreed? It has created a compliance scoring system with agreed-on standards. For example, a recurring issue is the matter of overtime beyond the factory's commitment versus the factory's need to meet production requirements. In Timberland's code, employees cannot work more than sixty hours per week. If it turns out that employees in a factory work more than sixty but fewer than seventy hours per week, it is deemed a low risk of unfair labor practices, and Timberland will not stop working with that plant. But that supplier's score will be lowered, which shows up in the Fair Factories database. If the number of hours goes beyond a threshold—for example, seventy hours per week—which creates a high risk, or if the supplier does not change its practices after repeated requests, Timberland will stop working with that supplier.

One of the biggest challenges organizations face in maintaining standards is to avoid exceptions and special cases. Timberland's policy is not to approve any supplier that has not gone through its own code-of-conduct assessment process. In order to guarantee compliance, Timberland's purchasing system will not allow a business unit manager to input details about a supplier until such an assessment has been undertaken. In this way, Timberland has aligned its standards of behavior with its principles by building in procedural safeguards to ensure adherence to its principles, even when a manager has an urgent business reason for seeking a waiver.

Create a Safe Space

For employees to trust in transparency, they must first feel safe physically, financially, and emotionally. There can be no fear of raising difficult issues or admitting mistakes; undue pressure and fear of losing one's job make these difficult or impossible. Transparency is also built on respect. Employees must feel they have a personal relationship with their leaders that allows them to be comfortable taking the risk of bringing up a touchy subject.

The first step to creating a safe place for the truth to be told is to be sure that senior leaders even know what the issue is. Several years ago, I was working with an international natural resources company to develop new ethics training. The general counsel proudly showed me the video-based training the company had been using. A module on sexual harassment showed a male employee inappropriately approaching a woman working on the factory floor. Over time, his interactions became more intimate and more uncomfortable for the woman. Finally, she reported the matter to her supervisor. The supervisor—obviously busy, his office piled to the ceiling with papers—barely gave her the time of day. E-mailing on his BlackBerry while speaking to her, he said, "Oh, that's just Bob being Bob. He doesn't mean anything by it." In the next scene, the woman's confidante told her that she needed to go to human resources or to the ethics officer to report the matter. She could not ignore it.

As the general counsel turned off the video, I asked him why he did not hold the supervisor responsible. The general counsel looked at me with a quizzical expression and replied, "The supervisor wasn't harassing the woman." It was then I knew the source of the problem for this organization: leadership did not yet understand what the real issue was. The immediate problem was a female employee being harassed, but the underlying problem was that frontline supervisors were not held responsible for creating an environment in which employees would feel comfortable raising difficult issues. In such an environment, it is difficult for the truth to be heard; transparency is thwarted.

The second step is to require leaders to affirmatively create safe spaces as opposed to only responding to violations. A safe place in which people feel comfortable raising issues requires more than freedom from retaliation. It requires the skills that Jim McNerney brought to Boeing: the ability to find out what has been making people afraid to raise issues or report misconduct.

Several years ago, I conducted a culture assessment for USZ, the global manufacturer. Because the organization was so large, we conducted focus groups in specific business units that scored in the upper 10 percent and the bottom 10 percent on their all-employee ethics climate surveys. The business unit with the top ethics score was an engineering group developing highly classified technology for the Pentagon and based in Washington, D.C. For this group, scoring high on the ethics survey meant that nearly everyone was familiar with the company's code of conduct and each person felt comfortable reporting misconduct if it were observed. Sure enough, when I met with these engineers and other professionals in focus groups, they reiterated that they took ethics seriously and would in fact report misconduct. One reason for their high standards, they told me, was that government officials were colocated in their offices, overseeing and collaborating on various aspects of their work. "Of course we would report misconduct!"

I then asked what I thought was a similar question: If they were going to be late or over budget delivering their commitments to the government that quarter, when would they tell their supervisor? Now they looked at me as if I had just sprouted another head. "If I had an issue, I would think long and hard before bringing it up," said one. Another told me that raising a potential problem that would damage their numbers would be a CLM—a career-limiting move. This group's supervisors were always busy and were not considered approachable on issues that would interfere with meeting their goals. As a result, these engineers policed themselves and would never bring bad news forward.

My next focus group was with those supervisors. I was curious to see what these busy tyrants looked like in person. However, instead of meeting with a bunch of hard-nosed prima donnas, I found myself sitting with a group of nice people who were under incredible pressure to perform. They were so busy each day dealing with a new set of emergencies that they had neither the time nor the interest to hear what was on their employees' minds, even if it could help them solve their own problems.

As I left the facility, I called my client with a warning that the survey data were wrong. This top-performing site was in fact one of the company's riskiest locations, a place where problems could easily become serious before exploding into the open.

In fact, such midlevel managers are often the demographic group within an organization that faces the greatest pressure. They can feel squeezed between carrying out edicts from the top and actually getting the job done. They are often frustrated, feeling that they are resource deprived and left without the ability to control their own fates. Senior leadership may be tasking them with profit-and-loss responsibility for their domains, yet they may not be able to control key inputs from suppliers—or even from other parts of the organization—that would directly affect their success. It is hardly likely that such frustrated and overstressed managers will have the time or inclination to provide a safe space in which uncomfortable truth can be told. They therefore create a major risk for unethical practices.

In addition, midlevel managers in many organizations have not had extensive leadership development training. Successful sales representatives or internal subject matter experts such as engineers are often promoted into leadership positions without regard to whether they can actually lead others. These managers may not have been provided with sufficient tools and training to manage the pressure and provide the empathetic reception that employees need if they have a problem to discuss.

The result is that line employees often feel their supervisors do not make it possible for them to raise issues or concerns. Even worse, supervisors in many organizations are themselves the source of the employees' fears, which makes it that much harder for senior leadership to create a culture in which truth can be heard. Dedicating limited training resources to helping midlevel managers be better at creating a safe place for issues to be raised might be the best investment an organization can make to ensure that potential problems and risks are raised as early as possible.

Don't Isolate Yourself

Every leader needs someone, like the medieval court jester, who has license to speak truth to power, bringing the king the bad news no one else dares deliver. One of the most persistent roadblocks to establishing an ethical culture is the isolation of leaders and their lack of adequate counsel on contrary opinions. When a person becomes a leader, there is a change in how people relate to him or her. Leaders may need to show confidence 100 percent of the time, but most often feel self-doubt and even fear. The last thing a leader needs is people focused on pleasing him or her for their own advantage rather than supplying the straight truth on a particular situation. While most leaders will be told of ethics problems once incidents have occurred, fewer are told of the culture tensions that may be breeding trouble. If it has not yet become a crisis, why bother the boss?

Leaders need to be overt in fighting this tendency by creating safe ways for others to report concerns or express contrary views. One model I have used successfully is to have the leader appoint a member of his or her team as the official devil's advocate for a particular meeting or project. This person is given formal permission to offer alternative perspectives, which often takes the discussion down a useful path that otherwise might have been closed off.

Similarly, when leaders go into the field to visit locations, they need opportunities to go off script and to have open dialogue with line employees and midlevel managers. One junior finance professional told me that one of the most productive meetings she ever had took place when the CFO popped into her cubicle, sat down, and said, "How are things going? What can I do to help?"

Get to the Heart of the Issue

Once an organization gains a deep understanding of the root causes of its barriers to performance, it is easy to focus on the core behaviors that require adjustment. Several years ago, an international beverage company asked me to develop ethics-awareness training. When organizations were first implementing standards and training to comply with the 2002 Sarbanes-Oxley legislation, they often focused on making sure that employees knew the proper processes and procedures. But they often overlooked whether employees would in fact adhere to the new standards. For this beverage company, one of the challenges was overcoming a hero culture. In a sales-oriented environment in which successes and failures were highly visible, it was seen as a sign

of weakness either to ask questions or not to know the proper procedures. As a result, the major theme of the training was not the rules
themselves but how to admit mistakes. We created scenarios that
permitted managers to speak openly with their direct reports about
their own mistakes, emphasizing that admitting a mistake or admitting
that one did not know the proper procedure was actually a sign of
strength.

In other organizations, creating transparency involved breaking
down other types of barriers. At Northern Defense, one of the biggest
barriers to performance was the difficulty that production managers
had in getting the parts and components they needed from their own
internal suppliers. Supply managers, sitting in a division headquarters,
needed to allocate components to production managers across the
organization while coordinating with procurement to ensure that there
was neither an oversupply nor an undersupply. At the other end of the
chain, the production managers needed to be sure they would have
enough components to get the product manufactured on schedule.

In most instances, the production managers had never met their
internal supply manager in person. Most of their communication was
by e-mail or telephone. Typically the anxious production manager
would demand that 100 percent of all the components needed be
shipped immediately. This created stress for the supply managers, who
were receiving similar calls from other production managers across the
organization. Each communication became a head-butting zero-sum
battle to obtain parts.

Finally, senior leadership brought the supply managers and the
production managers together. Once they had gotten to know each
other as people, relationships changed dramatically. Instead of trying
to win confrontational zero-sum games, the managers could engage in
personal relationships and develop trust and therefore transparency. If
a production manager asked for 100 percent of the parts immediately,
the supply manager could push back in a friendly way: "How many do
you really need, and when do you really need them?" The supply
manager could stagger deliveries to satisfy all of the production manag-

ers, and a production manager could trust that the supply manager wouldn't undermine his or her production delivery schedule.

At Western Financial, a similar approach helped address the continual stand-off between sales representatives and underwriters. When their relationship was only by e-mail or telephone, it was very difficult for either to understand or sympathize with the other's challenges. Sales reps were focused only on their own requirements, without understanding the challenges that an underwriter faced in obtaining approvals. A busy underwriter, supporting multiple sales reps, would naturally gravitate toward solving the problems of the people he or she knew best. Savvy sales managers and underwriting managers began to bring key teams together for periodic visits in order to build relationships. At first, the managers thought that they would bring underwriters to the field, where they could meet prospective customers and learn more about the sales reps' business practices. As it turned out, the solution was far simpler: the sales reps simply wanted to get to know the underwriters socially. Taking an underwriter out to a ball game or a local event proved to be far more effective in building relationships. Underwriters began to understand how each sales rep approached a particular case, which speeded up the approval process.

The organizations that embody transparency are not those that go overboard touting their organizational self-awareness. Instead, they are the ones that have pragmatically assessed the weakest links in the relationship chain that prevent the truth from being heard and have systematically developed interventions to close those gaps.

Your Plan for High Performance

There are numerous success stories of companies such as Timberland that have used the capabilities and resources supported by their cultures—bolstered by the power values—to meet tough business objectives. Other companies, such as Boeing, have reinvigorated their values to build a culture that lets them come back from a disaster or reclaim a leadership position. And some, such as Johnson & Johnson, have forgotten the importance of connecting their values to their brand—with sorry results.

Many companies with less cataclysmic issues evaluate their culture to determine whether they have competitive opportunities that they have not fully developed. As I outlined in Chapter One, issues lurking just below the surface could be at the heart of why your organization's strategy implementation and execution have been frustrating, why employees don't report questionable business practices, or why a new team or organization formed through a reorganization or acquisition is still struggling to get its footing.

Sometimes leaders have a gnawing sense of problems they can't put their finger on. Nothing is definitely wrong, but something doesn't feel right. To see whether culture misalignment is at the heart of the challenges you may be facing, you need a model and approach with which you can make your organization's culture an advantage and not an albatross. If we accept the principle that you cannot manage what you cannot measure, we need to break down the culture alignment process into measurable components so leaders can focus on the dimensions of culture that lend themselves to specific behaviors.

LOOKING FOR ALIGNMENT

High-performing cultures have the lowest amount of friction among their core elements: principles, goals, and standards. How do they do it? The only means by which an organization can achieve such alignment is through its employees. As I often tell my clients, "It's all about your people. Not because that's nice, but because they're what matters for the success you want." You know now that employees generally want to feel commitment and engagement toward their work and their company, so the more your company can clear the way for its people to work to their full abilities, the more efficient and effective their work will be and the fewer performance and ethical risks they are likely to take. Examining the interaction and coordination of your organization's principles, goals, and standards is the means by which you can discover the potential weak spots or hot spots that require intervention.

That is why it is important to understand the interactions among commitment, integrity, and transparency—the values that keep these core elements in sync (aligned) with each other. We have seen over and over what can happen when these cultural elements are at odds with each other.

Commitment links principles to goals by addressing how your people can bring their own principles to work. When those principles are aligned with your organization's goals, they feel a connection to the organization, which drives commitment. We saw this with the "RED leader" at The Gap in Chapter One and the Walmart managers in Chapter Five. Your organization can accelerate this process—making it easier for your people to bring their values to work—by creating opportunities for them to work autonomously and take ownership of their work.

Integrity links goals—what your organization strives to do—with its standards of behavior—how things are done. The organization can align its goals with its standards by insisting that its people do their jobs in a manner consistent with those goals. In parallel, the organization can ensure that both leaders and employees are "walking the talk" by insisting that people be accountable for their actions and making sure there are consequences for failing to live up to one's commitments. We saw this at Boeing in Chapter Three, when Jim McNerney revised the compensation system to make managers more accountable for behaviors he wanted to instill.

Transparency reveals how well your organization's standards align with its principles. Are you and your people acting according to your principles? In other words, are you being true to yourselves? If the standards are consistent with the principles, there is clarity in how the organization operates. And if employees are free to speak the truth, the organization can more easily discover where principles are in conflict and whether its own principles are really what you and other leaders proclaim them to be.

So how do you achieve alignment?

Jim Collins found that alignment is not something that successful leaders deal with explicitly.[1] Perhaps intuitively, they create the conditions in which engagement, alignment, and the ability to deal with change arise naturally. In these positive corporate cultures, employees can feel good about themselves and their work (commitment), they can raise issues and freely ask questions (transparency), and they do not feel challenged by unfair or inconsistent work processes, because people take personal responsibility for their actions and live up to their commitments (integrity).

But when some of the elements of culture are out of alignment, frustrations certainly occur. When the principles are not in alignment with the goals, employees disengage and feel less vested interest in their work (lack of commitment). When goals move out of sync with standards, unfairness arises as managers and employees "do what they have to do" rather than what they have said they would do (lack of integrity). And when standards are out of alignment with values, employees see that the organization's actions are not consistent with its principles and it becomes very difficult to ask uncomfortable but important questions and ensure that the truth is heard (lack of transparency).

Most organizations have problems with one, two, or all three of the alignment points that the power values affect. Many become quite adept at compensating for their weak spots. We saw at Western Financial, for example, that trust based on a charismatic leader's transparency—his willingness to admit when he was flying by the seat of his pants—had masked challenges to integrity brought on by inconsistent policies and processes, inconsistencies that might have been the root causes of the fraud the sales representatives engaged in. Similarly, as we will see later in this chapter, I found strong commitment on the part of Northern Defense employees, but it was also masking a dangerous lack of transparency—because employees would not raise questions and problems.

An organization seeking to develop an action plan to remove roadblocks must become aware of the root causes of its lack of alignment. We will now look at a three-step process—assessing, planning, and acting—that you can use to get at the root cause of a culture problem and then develop an action plan to nudge your organization's principles, goals, and standards into alignment:

1. *Assess.* As a leader, you must learn about your people and your culture in the context of their values and the performance roadblocks they face.
2. *Plan.* With all of the data in hand, the relationships among the elements of culture and the power values that align them can tell you what issues are at the root cause of your performance roadblocks and what behaviors will be at the heart of the solution.

3. *Act.* Design an action plan that allows behavior changes to progress logically and can be adapted for the specific needs of the subcultures inside your organization.

ASSESS

Does your organization know where it stands? While senior leaders may have an intuitive sense of where the culture-based problems lie, they may not know the depth of the issue and probably do not know how to begin fixing it. A formal assessment of the organization's culture and how the organization's principles, goals, and standards are aligned can take you a long way toward framing an action plan.

There is no one tool or instrument that can perform an "MRI" of a company's culture. There are too many moving parts. Instead, a culture assessment is the coordinated analysis of various forms of data, some of which the company may already be using and some of which need to be deployed just for this purpose. The data can take many forms, from surveys to anecdotes to interviews, but in all cases they must cover some key bases. Let's look at the methods available to you and your organization to gather the data needed to align your culture.

Principles and Beliefs

Many organizations have official statements of their core values by one name or another. Frankly, these are mostly irrelevant. What we are after here is the reality. An organization must understand the range of the unstated core values that its employees and managers embody. Leadership must create a map of the motivations and the fears of its people in order to include employees in the process of creating a more dynamic corporate culture. The most critical question is whether employees feel that their personal values are reflected in the organization's culture. This understanding is critical to gauge employees' levels of commitment and their ability or desire to step up and take ownership of issues they see inside the organization.

Personal Values

Surveys are one way to uncover employees' personal values. My prefer-
ence is to use a dedicated values assessment instrument that focuses on
specific values terms, such as those we saw in Chapter Three. Gleaning
values from more traditional employee engagement and climate surveys
is difficult because the questions focus on observation of the environment without looking more deeply at the reasons or causes that created
that situation. For example, some questions probe as to whether the
participant is satisfied with his or her job but may not get at the real
reasons why or what may be holding him or her back. It's like a doctor
asking you if you feel well or where it hurts and stopping there. A values
assessment can begin to probe at deeper motivations and beliefs that
guide behavior. When I conduct a values assessment and uncover
employees' personal values, I tell leadership that one way to look at the
results is to imagine that each employee has put a number of sticky
notes on his or her body like mini–sandwich boards, each naming a
value that the employee wants everyone else to know is important to
him or her. For example, an employee who lists "honesty" as a personal
value is really sending a message to leadership: "Honesty is important
to me—both my honesty and yours. Don't be dishonest with me, and
don't pressure me to be dishonest with you, with my coworkers, or with
our customers."

Organizational Values

Because culture is inherently subjective, there is no picture of what the
culture values objectively are. Instead, it is critical to get a sense of how
your people perceive their culture. For example, a manager may have
no wish to be manipulative, but if her employees feel manipulated,
that's a problem. If nothing else, it shows that this manager and her
people don't understand each other.

That said, various tools to assess values can provide you with an
objective set of measurements that are helpful in guiding the development of an action plan. My clients find it helpful to see the percentage
of the values their employees have chosen to describe the current

culture that are negative. When compared across the organization's key demographics—such as job function, job level, and location—this percentage can serve as a benchmark for gauging improvement as well as an indicator of which area of the organization needs the most attention.

What is on your employees' minds day in and day out? Is that what you would like them to be thinking about? Here, the "values" are the actual behaviors and motivations of employees, not their desired goals.

As I discussed in Chapter Three, some of the values that employees identify as making up the organization's culture will be negative. These indicate where employees feel frustrated and where there are compliance and performance risks, but also where performance opportunities may be waiting. Remember that culture drives performance. This means that all the organizational values you can identify, both positive and negative, are opportunities for you to boost your organization's performance.

Mission and Goals

In assessing the organization's goals from a culture perspective, you need to take two different perspectives: how your people evaluate the stated goals of the organization and its leaders and how they evaluate their own personal goals.

Organizational (Stated) Goals

The key question is whether leadership has articulated organizational goals in a manner that lends itself to action. The assessment process must uncover the challenges that your people face in drilling down from objectives to behaviors.

For example, when I ask leaders to define their organization's goals, they often start with broad strategic objectives such as, "We will be number one in our market." When I ask how the organization will achieve this goal, the answer is often another strategic objective, such as, "We will become number one by outcompeting the competition."

"Well, how will you do that?" I ask. I'll then get a reply such as, "We will lower our costs and therefore lower our prices." That's better, but it's still not actionable.

You need to translate your organization's strategic goals into very specific behaviors that each manager and employee can understand and engage in. If a manager is tasked, for example, with reducing production costs by 10 percent, she must decide how she will approach that challenge. Will she invite her team to participate in the process, enlisting them to develop their own ideas, or will she simply bark out her demands, causing her people to scramble and panic about what they need to do? In so many instances, employees know they need to work hard but truly do not understand what objectives they are supposed to be pursuing. Even for a broad goal such as outcompeting the competition, the specific behaviors will fall back into our familiar culture categories, such as taking responsibility and being accountable for making key decisions or creating an environment in which issues can be safely raised.

Personal and Informal Goals

It is equally important to assess how your people see their own personal goals within the organization. This takes two key forms. First, are compensation and incentives aligned with the organization's broader goals? That is, do employees' personal goals put them in line with or at odds with the organization's strategic objectives? We saw this challenge at Western Financial, for example, when sales representatives were compensated for bringing in as much new business (top-line revenue) as possible, even though that business might undermine profits (bottom-line revenue) down the road.

Second, are employees' personal goals focused on organizational issues at all? In some organizations, it is all employees can do to just get through the day. A personal goal may be nothing more aspirational than not getting laid off or not getting yelled at by the boss. The behaviors people engage in to achieve such goals are things like, "Do not cross so-and-so," and, "If I don't speak up, nobody will call me stupid."

These are hardly likely to be in alignment with—or to contribute much to—the company's strategic goals.

An assessment of goals will examine how well performance evaluations are aligned with the organization's goals. How are people compensated, and where do they feel conflicted? The place to start is the existing documents and procedures. Then it is time to go out into the field to ask the employees themselves. You might well learn things you would never have found out any other way. One manager got out from behind his desk and found out that a number of seemingly unsolvable operational problems were really not operational problems at all. The problem was that one employee in a key role was such a bully that other people avoided him as much as possible, however much more inefficient that made their work.

In many organizations, leaders have not looked at employees' intrinsic motivations as thoroughly as they have evaluated extrinsic motivators such as compensation. These leaders may be surprised to learn what really motivates their employees. The focus groups and interviews used to uncover employees' values will also reveal much about their personal goals.

Standards of Behavior

An assessment of standards looks at the alignment between what the organization is asking people to do and what they actually do. Here we need to determine the extent to which social norms are out of sync with stated standards of behavior. Your assessment of standards must be able to answer the following questions:

1. Where are there conflicts between stated policies and the way people actually do their work?
2. What—if any—are the means by which conflicting policies can be reconciled?
3. If there are conflicting ways of doing things, who is motivated to change the policies rather than "kicking the can down the road"?

For many organizations, this segment of the assessment begins with evaluations of existing processes and best practices. However, these evaluations often look at the desired best practice but not at the gap between what people are asked to do and what they are actually doing. In some organizations, this alignment challenge is relatively benign. There are multiple sets of policies and processes, and each employee is left to decide which process to follow in any particular instance. The assessment must be able to uncover how those decisions are made and the extent to which they create risks for the organization. But even if the misalignment is not causing problems now, frustrations will mount if it is not addressed. What happens when line employees see that following the strict letter of a production protocol reduces daily output; that their manager is unable to help, caught between her production goals and her responsibility to follow the rules; and that there never seems to be anyone around to ask for guidance?

The deeper challenge comes when social norms dictate behavior that runs contrary to official standards and desired practices. There may be such peer pressure to conform to the social norm that serious mistakes go unreported. I once worked with an auto manufacturer that used the famous Toyota production system. "Team members" on the assembly line were trained to be responsible for the parts they used. Everyone was empowered to act as an inspector for his or her own work and for that of coworkers. When a problem on any vehicle was spotted, any team member could halt production by pulling a rope—called an *andon* cord—strung along the assembly line. Only when the problem was resolved would the line be restarted.

This process empowered every team member to monitor the quality of every car produced. What could be a better strategy to ensure quality? But workers felt tremendous pressure *not* to pull that cord. No supervisor would ever tell any worker not to, but everyone knew that slowing down the line could mean forced overtime on Saturday to make up for lost production time. That would cost the managers their metrics and cost the worker who pulled the cord and his or her coworkers a precious day off. Pull the cord at your peril.

An effective assessment must take into account any available data—from employee and customer surveys to accident or defect investigations—that might reveal or suggest the gaps between what people are supposed to do and what they actually do. Then there need to be interviews or other types of anecdotal evaluation to learn as much as possible about these gaps.

Status of Commitment, Integrity, and Transparency

In addition to gathering data about the culture, you need to conduct an assessment of the status of the 3 power values. No matter whether your organization uses the same terminology of *"integrity," "commitment,"* and *"transparency,"* you need to know how well these concepts are known in the organization, if at all. An objective values assessment, targeted interviews, and focus groups can all shed light on the status of the power values.

Integrity

To what extent do employees perceive consistency, fairness, and accountability in the organization's culture? In addition to values assessments, leaders can look at the qualitative nature of ethics complaints and investigations, as well as previous efforts to determine how decisions are made within the organization. Who reviews decisions? Are people supported when they make decisions for which they are authorized? If so, how are they supported?

Commitment

The status of commitment can be determined by looking at the extent to which the culture includes behaviors that support connection and autonomy. An employee's sense of connection to the organization can be evaluated through traditional human resource practices such as conducting engagement surveys or evaluating retention levels. If the surveys are comprehensive, autonomy can be evaluated through these same means so that leaders can identify the workforce's intrinsic motivations.[2] Why do people love their jobs? When employees are interviewed about their motivations, the drivers of commitment include factors such as achieving a personal sense of accomplishment and feeling good about being part of a successful team.

Transparency

To what extent do employees perceive clarity of corporate purpose in all activities? To what extent do they feel able to tell the truth, raise issues, and ask questions? Here, external data can be helpful. How do customers perceive the company and its reputation? What aspects of the organization and its products do they like or dislike? What aspects of the organization earn respect or disdain? How do external watchdogs such as consumer agencies and environmental groups see the organization?

Subcultures

Many of these questions need to be asked for each of the organization's subcultures—its business units and divisions, its functions and hierarchical levels, its age cohorts and geographical locations. For example, when I conduct values assessments, I look for variations in perceptions among key constituencies that need to work together. Do managers see the world differently from the people who report to them? If so, how? Does the sales organization have a different outlook from that of the people back at the home office, whether the home office is underwriting for an insurance company or contracting and procurement for a manufacturing company?

PLAN

With slews of data in hand, leadership can begin to create a sense of order from what may at first seem like a mass of complaints from peevish employees. It is time to develop a plan, prioritizing the issues and then understanding the causal connections between the challenges that have been uncovered. For example, we have seen the differences between organizations in which lack of transparency affects integrity (Johnson & Johnson) and in which lack of integrity affects transparency (BP). Going deeper, leaders must also understand which issues are at the root of their roadblocks to performance. For example, an organization that is losing credibility because its business conduct lacks integrity may trace its problem to poor processes. But another organization with a similar symptom might find that the root cause is poor communications and its managers' fundamental lack of respect for their employees.

I use a three-step process to analyze the building blocks of culture you have assessed, make some order out of it, and come up with an actionable plan:

1. *Identify the desired culture.* I often recommend starting with a look at the values that employees believe are essential for the organization to be high performing. These values can offer not only insights into the direction employees feel the organization should go but, more important, also into the hurdles that the organization must overcome to create a fully engaged workforce. When employees articulate the values needed for the organization to be high performing, they tend to be more pragmatic and behavior driven than senior leaders, who see the company's performance from the vantage point of strategy. Whereas leaders may be thinking "innovation," "customer focus," or even "efficiency," employees are often thinking that more basic values such as "employee appreciation," "best practices," and "open communication" may be required.

2. *Identify the culture gaps.* Look for the gaps between the goals that leaders state and the goals that employees perceive and between the principles and beliefs that leadership considers necessary and the principles and beliefs that employees are bringing to the table.

3. *Identify the relevant power values.* Test each of the power values to determine which desired behaviors are primary and which are dependent on some other behavior happening first.

A look at how two organizations developed a strategic plan to remove roadblocks to performance will provide insight into how to approach the challenges in your own organization.

Northern Defense

Remember Northern Defense, the U.S.-based division of a global manufacturing and aerospace company that was coping with the changes in the defense industry as the Iraq and Afghanistan wars were winding down in 2010? Northern had implemented programs efficiently and seen steady growth for twenty years, but now had to identify new opportunities and venture into new markets. Leadership wanted to be sure that there was nothing systemic in Northern's culture that would impede this transition and that the company could be as innovative as they knew it would need to be.

Values Assessment

The assessment revealed the status of Northern Defense's culture.

Goals: Employees were becoming confused about the corporate mission. When Northern was solely a defense company, employees felt an extra sense of commitment, knowing that their products and services were serving soldiers in the field. But as Northern began to acquire commercial companies as part of its diversification, that sense of mission became diluted. For many employees, "getting product out" had become the company's only goal.

Standards: When the legacy companies that were rolled into Northern Defense still operated independently, the chain of command within each facility had been clear. There were directives to follow and people to go to when instructions didn't make sense. But as the company grew and its structure became more complex, employees no longer knew where to go for help when processes and procedures conflicted. "Even my boss can't tell me what I'm supposed to do" became a common frustration throughout the company.

Principles: The employees at Northern Defense embodied values at the communal level of awareness. They wanted to feel as deeply connected to the organization as they always had, but now they were feeling that those communal-level values were no longer present in a culture dominated by the need to get product out the door.

The Power Values

There seemed to be considerable challenges within each of the three elements of culture. In any large organization, that is normal. What Northern Defense's leadership and I didn't know yet was how significant these challenges were in terms of risks and in terms of performance. The assessment therefore went deeper, examining how the 3 power values were situated to serve as catalysts for culture alignment:

Commitment: In general, the employees at Northern Defense were quite engaged. They had a powerful need to belong to something greater than themselves and always looked to their leaders to create a compelling vision of which they could be part. Veteran employees had always felt that the products would go out the door regardless of what corporate did because each employee had a strong personal commitment to the soldier in the field. But younger employees did not feel the same commitment. An attitude of "that's not my job" had begun to put individuals' goals ahead of the organization's goals.

Integrity: Principles and standards were not in alignment due to perceptions of favoritism and inconsistency in how projects and assignments were delegated. There were too many procedures to follow, and confusion concerning the chain of command left employees unsure who was supposed to do what. In turn, local "warlords" took advantage of that leadership vacuum, running their departments however they needed to in order to get the job done.

Transparency: With such serious changes afoot, it was not clear to employees how well Northern Defense was living its values. Because of the pressure to deliver, employees were worried about quality. They could no longer feel confident that what the organization did was in line with the perceived but unstated values of serving soldiers and delivering the highest-quality product. Employees' negativity about their jobs was clouding their broader view of the organization. They were increasingly hesitant to raise issues with pressured and nervous managers who clearly did not want to hear bad news. One employee said, "If you don't ask questions, no one will think you're stupid," and many others felt the same way.

Bringing Elements of the Culture into Alignment
With these data on Northern Defense's culture—the individual and collective beliefs and behaviors—in hand, the company's leaders evaluated their options for cultural alignment.

Identify the Desired Culture: When Northern Defense had been busy with multiple defense projects, getting product out the door at the highest quality and the lowest price had been the key to success. Leaders sought a culture in which operations ran smoothly. Employees would know what they needed to do and would feel safe raising questions when they did not or if they found something amiss.

But Northern Defense's leaders needed a different type of culture for a new era, one that inculcated innovation and adaptability. Business development leaders needed engineers and project managers to be creative in developing new approaches, not only to meet the unanticipated needs of military customers but also to develop new products and services that could be adapted to the commercial market. Employees at all levels needed to be able to take more risks. The company needed thinkers willing to take chances in proposing new ideas that might be crazy but might, in an open environment, lead to real breakthroughs.

Identify the Culture Gaps: Adaptability showed the greatest gap between the values employees saw in the culture around them and the values they felt were essential for Northern's high performance. For employees, adaptability was directly related to the fear that Northern was not nimble enough to respond to new opportunities and challenges, that is, to survive for the long run. Employees' perceptions that the organization was mired in bureaucracy and reactive firefighting reinforced their perceptions that their leaders could not provide a future direction.

When I analyzed the values assessment of managers and supervisors, I learned more about what it would take to bridge some of these gaps. The values that managers were most eager to see in the culture were "collaboration" and "coaching/mentoring"; supervisors were looking for "teamwork" and "adaptability." Together what they wanted was not greater power but better ways to work with each other.

When Northern's leaders and I put the puzzle pieces together, we could see that the organization was looking for clarity as to how it should do its business better, that is, with more consistency and accountability. All of the power values were needed. Alignment through integrity would be critical to start. First the organization needed to begin operating efficiently, and standards needed to be consistently applied. But how was the organization going to engage its workers (building commitment) and dispel mistrust through open and honest communication (transparency)?

Identify the Relevant Power Values: The values assessment provided clues as to where to start. The assessment's most critical insight was that teamwork would be the key to integrity. Many leaders have thought for years that the key to consistent business practices is to develop disciplined quality and Six Sigma programs. But in many instances, the solution to a process problem is not more process. At Northern Defense, it was not so much inefficient processes as the lack of effective teamwork that was hobbling performance, since so much work depended on close interaction with others in different parts of the organization. Inconsistent processes and procedures were becoming problems, not because the processes were inherently faulty, but because people weren't talking with one another. As part of its cost-saving efforts, Northern had cut back on meetings that could not be directly billed to a project and a customer, and regional meetings had been cancelled altogether. People who needed to work together were not meeting one another.

When we dug down to the deepest level, we found that one reason for the poor teamwork was a perceived lack of leadership. Northern's employees valued close interaction with their leaders, so they hated the matrixed organizational structure—a result of the company's growth—

in which managers were off-site and had only indirect responsibility and oversight. Employees were looking for their leaders to lead, but the executive staff was often too remote to have much impact on any given facility. Many employees had no personal relationship with their senior leaders and no idea of those leaders' personal expectations. Leadership was lacking at the local level as well. Busy supervisors who had never had effective management training made employees feel that they were not being spoken to honestly; this was creating stress in the workplace and confusion about the integrity of the work objectives.

Now leadership was able to develop a plan. Northern needed to get its leaders and managers at all levels out of their offices and cubicles and out into the field. Senior leaders needed to have more of a presence in the field locations, and local leaders were given instructions and training on how to ensure that supervisors and midlevel managers were taking responsibility for their actions and engaging in more productive communications with individual contributors.

Western Financial

Let's look at another example of what a plan can look like, this time for a financial services organization.

Western Financial had been very successful over the previous ten years selling insurance and annuity packages to independent brokers and financial planners. The company's knowledgeable sales representatives had created strong relationships with the independent brokers and financial planners who sold its products to their own clients. Nevertheless, the market had been signaling for some time that Western Financial's products were becoming dated; the brokers and plan managers wanted online access and more sophisticated tools in order to take full advantage of those products. So the sales reps were now demanding that their company come up with new technology to keep its product line competitive. In addition, Western Financial was trying to uncover any cultural factors that might have contributed to the fraud committed by its sales reps in submitting false customer data to underwriters.

Values Assessment

The values assessment of Western Financial provided this snapshot of its culture.

Goals: At Western Financial there was one goal: winning. Failure was not an option and there was real fear; it was common knowledge (although not necessarily true) that "two years of not meeting goal and you're out." Leaders would tell me that they had never fired anyone for not making goal, yet they were happy that the threat seemed real to their employees. In fact, a significant percentage of reps didn't make goal, and some of those would leave of their own accord.

The lack of clarity as to whether Western Financial's success was (or should be) based on top-line or bottom-line revenues was sending deep reverberations throughout the company. Employees felt that the relationship between the field and home staffs would be determined by how this issue was articulated.

Standards: There were strong perceptions that the end-of-year rush to generate business in order to meet goal was creating tremendous inconsistency in approval criteria. Sales representatives were increasingly frustrated in not being able to predict how an underwriter would review an application. It seemed that early in the year, underwriting would approve cases only with terms so conservative that sales reps couldn't sell them. But at the end of the year, it seemed that underwriters would approve anything just to get the sale in the door. The general notion was that the organization was desperate to make its numbers and therefore too many decisions were being made as exceptions to the rules.

Principles and Beliefs: Western Financial employees were motivated by these values:

- A need to be appreciated and recognized
- An opportunity to have ownership of their particular area of expertise or responsibility
- A desire to feel that they were making a difference to the customers they served

- The personal challenges of completing difficult tasks and overcoming obstacles
- A need to feel included and a knowledge that leadership was "watching their backs"

Western Financial employees embodied these personal values and wanted to see them in their workplace. When they did, they could shine and feel fully engaged and motivated. But when they didn't, they felt frustrated and began to emotionally withdraw.

The Power Values
The assessment explored the status of the 3 power values at Western Financial.

Commitment: Lack of empowerment was becoming a growing frustration. Independent and well-educated employees wanted more autonomy. They knew what their customers needed and were willing to be held accountable if they didn't succeed. But they wanted to do it their own way. These feelings generated uncertainty about how to meet the goals and about what type of employee would be best suited to do so: a team player or a lone wolf.

We often think of team players as the ones who are engaged and committed, who take personal responsibility for the organization's success. They will go the extra mile for their organization because their goals and the organization's goals are one and the same. The key to fostering this kind of employee commitment is to ensure that employees feel that bringing their personal values to work is not a risk. Rather, it must be part of the culture.

At Western Financial, one of those values was autonomy—owning one's own work. People wanted more. But for a leader, granting someone more autonomy means delegating some of your own, and this is not easy. While many leaders say they want their people to take more responsibility, managers struggle with giving up control. Leadership at Western Financial saw that they would have to take small steps. Each manager was not only directed but required to determine which decisions and matters could in fact be delegated down. "None" was not an acceptable answer. Managers then needed to support their people when they made independent decisions based on that new authority. Senior leaders would question those managers to make sure they were delegating and supporting.

Integrity: Employees were asking the company to reconcile conflicting procedures so there would be consistency and predictability. For example, the employees saw the lack of clarity about guidelines for underwriting decisions in the second quarter versus the fourth quarter as a sign of weakened integrity. They were looking for clear and enforced consequences for not following agreed-on standards of conduct. If underwriting guidelines were going to change during the year, then the changes themselves should at least be more predictable. Lack of consistency and consequences was the culture factor behind the fraudulent applications as well. Sales reps who had allowed their hubris to cloud their judgment saw the lack of clear guidelines as an opportunity, thinking that no one would find the false data. These sales reps not only thought that the proverbial door to the safe was open; they actually thought they were being invited in.

More collaborative working relationships between sales and underwriting were needed to reduce distrust and align goals. More integrated and aligned teams would foster better strategizing on how to secure more business. To reduce frustrations caused by lack of responsiveness, several managers wanted sales and underwriting leadership to establish clear and objective guidelines and deadlines for responding to various types of inquiry and internal requests and then hold field and home office employees accountable for not fulfilling those guidelines or meeting those deadlines.

Transparency: Key leaders at various levels needed to build trusting relationships. Western's success had been largely due to the staff's trust in its senior leaders. Maintaining this trust in the face of change would require active attention. Leadership had to keep an eye on what was not happening as well as what was. That is, they had to be aware and take action when employees did not feel comfortable raising issues with their supervisors or when there was a gap between what leadership thought it was saying and how that message was being heard in the field.

To build institutional trust, the sales representatives needed to develop personal relationships with the underwriters. If they were going to work together as team, they needed to get to know one another and learn each other's motivations and values so they could give each other a greater degree of trust and goodwill during their daily interactions.

Bringing Elements of the Culture into Alignment

Now Western Financial needed to think about how the elements of its culture could be brought into better alignment.

Identify the Desired Culture: When I asked the employees at Western Financial during the values assessment which values were essential for the organization to perform at its highest potential, they chose "coaching/mentoring" more than any other. Coaching and mentoring? At first blush, that seemed to have come out of left field. What did that have to do with all the problems we had been bringing to light? But it became apparent in interviews that employees at all levels were seeking more skills to be able to better navigate the challenges in getting their work done. This highly educated workforce was looking for more empowerment (commitment) so that they could make decisions themselves and resolve the challenges in the underwriting and approval process.

Identify the Culture Gaps: This desire for the skills of empowerment had been put forth by leaders in order to address the deeper issue of the inconsistent implementation of Western Financial's business practices. Employees had been willing to put up with the inconsistencies because of the high degree of trust that most of the veteran employees had in the senior leadership team. Remember that as the company grew, these charismatic leaders had always been there for their people.

Identify the Relevant Power Values: The core of the challenges that Western Financial faced was in the perception that exceptions were the rule and that there was no telling how decisions would be made.

Accountability was the true underlying issue. Therefore, along with the workforce's request for consistency came a strong request that leadership promote accountability by implementing consequences for anyone who did not meet his or her commitments.

ACT

With your strategic approach in place, you can develop specific steps to implement your plan and bring your culture into alignment. There are two key approaches to implementing the action plan:

- Build up from the lower levels of values awareness.
- Stay as local as possible.

Build Up from the Lower Levels of Values Awareness

As Chapter Three showed, it won't help for leaders to encourage values at the communal level of awareness (such as collaboration or making a difference in the world) if employees are grappling with fundamental fears such as losing their jobs. In general, leaders need to systematically look at risk factors from each of the foundational levels of awareness to determine whether those factors are inhibiting performance. They then need to address those factors by promoting values at the next-higher level of awareness.

If the values assessment indicates that employees are struggling at the survival level of awareness (level 1), leaders need to focus on effective communication and relationship building (level 2) in order to assuage those fears. Sometimes leaders think that if employees are fearful, giving them positive news will help the situation. The opposite is true: employees do not want sugarcoated promises; they want the truth. Therefore, when organizations are addressing survival issues, open communication can be the best medicine.

When the relationship level of awareness (level 2) is generating problems, as in organizations that are rife with blame or in which leaders create their own fiefdoms, top leadership needs to establish clear processes that ensure fairness and accountability; that is, at the performance level of awareness (level 3). We saw this in the story of Mike and the safety guard in Chapter Four. Mike's immediate higher-ups, Paul and Richard, had "taken the law into their own hands" by refusing to use the new safety guard and teaching new employees not to use it. Their own leaders needed to hold them accountable for enforcing companywide safety practices, particularly those required by the Occupational Safety and Health Administration.

When employees are bogged down by poor processes, as in organizations where confusion, bureaucracy, inconsistency, or firefighting are dominant values in the culture, leadership needs not only to create consistency (level 3), but also to generate greater responsibility by focusing on the engagement level of awareness (level 4). For example, when something is seen as "bureaucratic," the perception is that systems are not working well and no one is taking responsibility for decisions and actions. Sometimes this perception is valid, and the organization does need to streamline and improve its business practices. But in many situations, the perception of bureaucracy grows out of employees' sense of helplessness to take control of their own workload or the projects for which they are responsible. Delegating responsibility is often the best way to address challenges at the performance level of awareness. Giving people a sense of ownership of an issue will engage them in finding a solution.

At Northern Defense, the survival level of awareness was not an issue, at least not in the near or medium term. Employees were not overly concerned about their immediate job security, despite the reduction in the number of projects as a result of the reductions in U.S. defense spending. They were hopeful that the company could survive any downturn. They were more concerned about blame and a perceived lack of respect (relationship level of awareness). Leadership identified the locations and business units that seemed to have the most trouble maintaining positive relations. Leaders in those areas were given the mandate to fix the problem by developing employee appreciation solutions that would resonate with those employees. Rather than relying on a corporate communications program or imposing mandatory training, leaders engaged supervisors in the process of developing better communication styles with their employees. Scripted talking points were used to help guide supervisors in conversations with their employees about what kind of communications worked best for them and what particular challenges they faced. In addition, plant leadership in key facilities was directed to provide specific intervention for the supervisors who had the worst reputations for seeding a culture of blame and recrimination.

The core issues that Northern Defense's leadership identified in the values assessment process were the compromised role of teamwork and its effect on the organization's ability to get its work done, and the employees' need to see that their leaders were leading. The executive staff began a program of spending extra time in the field. Moving beyond town hall meetings and periodic visits, the CEO insisted that business unit heads spend one week each month on location in order to develop deeper relationships with the local staff. At the facilities in which there had been gaps between engineering and production, mostly due to the lack of face-to-face contact, production and design teams were given opportunities to spend more physical time together.

In-person collaboration is expensive, which was one reason it had been cut back in recent years. However, once leadership saw the extent of the negative impact that poor teamwork was having on productivity, the business benefit of developing better teamwork became clear. Having the leaders be more accessible allowed employees to feel more comfortable asking informal questions and bouncing ideas off their leaders rather than having to make requests through e-mails or formal project management protocols. Having leaders be more visible and more engaged in the group's day-to-day operations also meant that decisions could be made more quickly and leaders felt more comfortable delegating decisions to local managers and employees with whom they now had personal and trusting relationships.

This benefit of deeper collaboration went to the core of the business as well. As leadership evaluated the need for two key business units to work better together, it decided to consolidate them into one unit. Groups that had been generating confusion because of their overlapping responsibilities were now collaborating and sharing best practices. Being part of the same business unit gave people throughout the organization more of an opportunity to meet informally and share ideas and ways of addressing problems.

Stay as Local as Possible

The secret for engaging employees in the process of aligning culture is to engage them in the process. Making the managers and employees most directly involved with the problem responsible for finding the solution ensures that the solution will be more effective than if it were handed down from corporate by managers who don't know how things really work in the field. One of the benefits of a values assessment is that knowing which values are important to employees helps leadership secure their buy-in. Leaders can simply tell their people: "We heard you, and we want you to develop the means to live the values you choose." If leaders acknowledge the values that their employees feel will make the organization high performing and then engage those employees in developing programs that support those values, the employees will naturally be engaged and committed.

As leaders evaluated the various roadblocks in Western Financial's culture, they focused on the inconsistent application of policies and the perception that there were no consequences for failing to follow through on commitments. Western Financial was clearly at a cultural crossroads. The ways in which leaders had sustained their culture in the past, through charisma and caring, were being strained as a younger workforce came in and as ever increasing pressure to perform had stretched the leaders' credibility to the limit. At first, Western Financial's divisional leadership thought that it would resolve these conflicts by focusing on increasing the trust in leadership that had worked so well in the past. Plans were put in place for leaders to spend more time in the field and develop closer relationships with their far-flung personnel. However, the leadership at Western Financial's parent company had a different plan in mind. They decided to bring in new leadership for Western Financial.

Of course, employees couldn't possibly have the trust in this brand-new team that they had had in their previous leaders. The new leadership understood the specific culture challenges in building consistency and consequences at Western Financial, with its particular history and mix of employees. They therefore focused on tightening up the challenges to integrity that were the root cause of the frustrations leading to lack of engagement and trust. Developing these new relationships was going to take time. The new leaders began the process of earning trust by engaging employees in the process of untangling knotty business processes and listening to what employees could see was needed to ensure smooth operations. Trusting that Western Financial's employees really did have their business's best interests at heart, the new leaders could be more open to seeing the logic of the solutions their people suggested.

SELF-AWARENESS

In Chapter One, I made an analogy between the difficulty leaders face in changing an organization's culture and the difficulty an individual faces in making a behavioral change such as losing weight or quitting smoking. As I noted, personal behavioral change is rarely hampered by not knowing what one should do. The organizational equivalent of the obvious "eat less and exercise more" is the equally obvious "engage employees more and give them less reason to be frustrated." Neither piece of advice tends to accomplish much by itself. So to make these notoriously difficult changes, both you and your people need to develop enough self-awareness to understand what will motivate change. Self-awareness—understanding what motivates us and what hinders us—is at the core of creating cultures that can outperform the competition by ensuring that employees are comfortable, confident, and able to work to their highest potential. For employees, self-awareness is a way to better understand how their human vulnerabilities play out in the workplace and how to withstand those pressures. For leaders, self-awareness is a way to make culture alignment much easier because you know where you need to start.

BP and Johnson & Johnson struggled through business challenges that others handled more easily because both lacked self-awareness. They were not conscious of some of their own most potent unstated values—both positive and negative. Relying on a facade of stated principles—Johnson & Johnson's Credo and BP's Operations Academy and operating management system—created dangerous vulnerability to self-deception, rationalization, and disengagement.

Successful organizations are those that do not try to sculpt the culture that leaders feel they need in order to meet market challenges. Goals and business challenges will change and the culture will need to adapt. Instead, successful companies focus on the dependable means by which they will travel down that unseen path. As an environment changes, it is not the perfectly adapted organism but the most adaptable organism that will survive. If an organization can focus on clearing the way for its talented employees to do their work, the journey will be as successful as it can be.

Safe travels.

NOTES

Chapter One

1. Kimes, M. "Why J&J's Headache Won't Go Away." *Fortune*, Aug. 19, 2010.

2. As Johnson & Johnson states on its public Web site (http://www.jnj.com/connect/about-jnj/jnj-credo): "The values that guide our decision making are spelled out in Our Credo. Put simply, Our Credo challenges us to put the needs and well-being of the people we serve first. Robert Wood Johnson, former chairman from 1932 to 1963 and a member of the Company's founding family, crafted Our Credo himself in 1943, just before Johnson & Johnson became a publicly traded company. This was long before anyone ever heard the term 'corporate social responsibility.' Our Credo is more than just a moral compass. We believe it's a recipe for business success. The fact that Johnson & Johnson is one of only a handful of companies that have flourished through more than a century of change is proof of that."

3. Testimony before the U.S. House, Committee on Oversight and Government Reform. Quoted in Bartz, S. "Johnson & Johnson's Motrin Recall Cover Up," May 28, 2010, americanfraud.blogspot http://americanfraud.blogspot.com/2010_05_01_archive.html.

4. The companies to which I refer by fictionalized names are actual clients with which I have worked and choose to remain anonymous.

5. Edgar Schein, the guru of organizational culture, defines culture in an anthropological manner: "A pattern of shared basic assumptions that was learned by a group as it solved its problems of external adaptation and internal integration, that has worked well enough to be considered validated, therefore, to be taught to new members as the correct way to perceive, think, and feel in relation to those problems." Schein, E. *Organizational Culture and Leadership.* San Francisco: Jossey-Bass, 2004.

6. Barrett, R. *Cultural Capital: A Fundamental Driver of Financial Performance.* Asheville, N.C.: Barrett Values Centre, Feb. 2010.

7. Ibid.

8. *2007 National Business Ethics Survey.* Washington, D.C.: Ethics Resource Center, 2007, p. 12.

9. This is not as sinister as it may sound. Employees may, for example, learn to be more accountable as the corporate culture becomes more customer facing and its people are called on to solve customer problems themselves rather than wait for some higher authority to do so.

10. "Timberland Responsibility," http://responsibility.timberland.com/climate/#reduce-footprint.

11. Collins, J. *Built to Last.* New York: HarperBusiness, 1994, p. 73.

12. Collins, J. "Aligning Action and Values." June 2000, http://www.jimcollins.com/article_topics/articles/aligning-action.html.

13. Kaplan, R. S., and Norton, D. P. "Measuring the Strategic Readiness of Intangible Assets." *Harvard Business Review*, Feb. 2004, 52–63.

14. Collins, J. *Good to Great.* New York: HarperCollins, 2001.

15. Kimes. "Why J&J's Headache Won't Go Away."

16. Singer, N., and Abelson, R. "Can Johnson & Johnson Get Its Act Together?" *New York Times*, Jan. 16, 2011.

Chapter Two

1. "BP's Hayward, in BBC Interview, States the Obvious," Nov. 9, 2010, FuelFix, http://fuelfix.com/blog/2010/11/09/bp%E2%80%99s-hayward-in-bbc-interview-states-the-obvious/.

2. "MIT Program Focuses on Operations Safety." *MIT News*, Apr. 10, 2008, http://web.mit.edu/newsoffice/2008/bp-mit-0410.html.

3. Elkind, P. "The Untold Story of the BP Oil Disaster." *Fortune*, Feb. 2, 2011, pp. 105–132.

4. *The Report of the BP U.S. Refineries Independent Safety Review Panel*, Jan. 2007, p. 60, http://www.bp.com/liveassets/bp_internet/globalbp/globalbp _uk_english/SP/STAGING/local_assets/assets/pdfs/Baker_panel _report.pdf.

5. Tenbrunsel, A. E., Diekmann, K. A., Wade-Benzoni, K. A., and Bazerman, M. H. "The Ethical Mirage: A Temporal Explanation as to Why We Aren't as Ethical as We Think We Are." Harvard Business School working paper 08–012, 2007.

6. Mazar, N., Amit, O., and Ariely, D. "The Dishonesty of Honest People: A Theory of Self-Concept Maintenance." *Journal of Marketing Research*, 2008, *45*, 633–644.

7. Tenbrunsel, A. E., and Messick, D. M. "Ethical Fading: The Role of Self-Deception in Unethical Behavior." *Social Justice Research*, 2004, *17*(2), 223–236.

8. Lyall, S. "In BP's Record, a History of Boldness and Costly Blunders." *New York Times*, July 12, 2010.

9. Ibid.

10. Shefrin, H., and Cervellati, E. M. "BP's Failure to Debias: Underscoring the Importance of Behavioral Corporate Finance." Working paper, Mar. 29, 2011, http://papers.ssrn.com/sol3/papers.cfm?abstract_id=1769213.

11. Tversky, A., and Kahneman, D. "Rational Choice and the Framing of Decisions." *Journal of Business*, 1986, *59*, 251–278.

12. Keltner, D. "The Power Paradox." *Greater Good*, Winter 2007–2008, http://greatergood.berkeley.edu/article/item/power_paradox/.

13. Asch, S. E. "Opinion and Social Pressure." *Scientific American*, Nov. 1955, pp. 33–35.

14. From the Federal Second Circuit Court decision ruling on Bernie Ebbers's appeal of his conviction. U.S. v. Bernard J. Ebbers, 458 F.3d 110. 2006.

15. Baard, P., Deci, E., and Ryan, R. "Intrinsic Need Satisfaction: A Motivational Basis of Performance and Well-Being in Two Work Settings." *Journal of Applied Psychology*, 2004, *34*, 2045–2068.

16. Milgram, S. *Obedience to Authority: An Experimental View*. New York: HarperCollins, 1974.

Chapter Three

1. Bain, D. Speech at the Boeing Leadership Meeting, Jan. 5, 2006, Orlando, Fla., http://community.seattletimes.nwsource.com/archive/?date=2006 0131&slug=boeingtranscript31.

2. "Why Boeing's Culture Breeds Turmoil." *BusinessWeek*, Mar. 21, 2005, http://www.businessweek.com/magazine/content/05_12/b3925039_mz011.htm.

3. "Straight Talk." *Boeing Frontiers*, 2004, *3*(2), http://www.boeing.com/news/frontiers/archive/2012/january/#/1/.

4. Richard Barrett, whose work I reference later in this chapter and throughout the rest of the book, offers this explanation for Maslow's importance: "Abraham Maslow was one of the first psychologists to draw our attention to needs-based motivation. In *Motivation and Personality* and *Toward a Psychology of Being*, Maslow proposed that humans operate as if they had a hierarchy of needs. The primary human need is survival. When we are able to master survival, we shift the focus of our consciousness to the establishment of relationships that make us feel safe. When we are able to master the art of relationship building, we shift the focus of our consciousness to satisfying our need for self-esteem. When we are able to feel a strong sense of self-worth, we shift the focus of our consciousness to self-actualization—overcoming the fears we hold that are preventing us from becoming viable and independent human beings. During self-actualization we learn to release the fears that keep us trapped in our dependency based 'we-ness' so that we can be free. This is the state of consciousness that I have called 'transformation.' The process of transformation corresponds to the process that Carl Jung termed individuation, and the process Roberto Assagioli termed psychosynthesis." "Origins of the Seven Levels of Consciousness Model," prepared by Richard Barrett, Barrett Values Centre, 2005. Used by permission.

5. The Barrett Seven Levels of Consciousness model describes the evolutionary development of human consciousness. It applies to all individuals and human group structures, such as organizations, communities, and nations. "Barrett Model: Seven Levels of Consciousness." http://www.valuescentre.com/culture/?sec=barrett_model.

6. McNerney, J. Speech to the Conference Board, Apr. 27, 2006, http://www.boeing.com/news/speeches/2006/mcnerney_060427.html.

7. Holmes, S. "Cleaning Up Boeing." *BusinessWeek*, Mar. 13, 2006, http://www.businessweek.com/magazine/content/06_11/b3975088.htm.

8. Ibid.

9. Barrett, R. *Liberating the Corporate Soul*. Burlington, Mass.: Butterworth-Heinemann, 1998. Barrett, R. *Building a Values-Driven Organization*. Burlington, Mass.: Butterworth-Heinemann, 2006.

10. Although speaking up requires individual courage, it is a social act with a social or organizational purpose.

11. Holmes, S. "Cleaning Up Boeing."

12. Collins, J. *Good to Great*. New York: HarperCollins, 2001, p. 21.

13. Developed by Barrett Values Centre, www.valuescentre.com.

14. Joan Shafer noted in discussions with me that in 2010, she conducted research on 139,000 employees who participated in corporate values assessments using the Barrett Values Centre's tools. These employees represented 170 organizations globally. Honesty, commitment, and positive attitude were the most frequently chosen personal values.

15. For example, revenues grew four times faster in strong cultures than in weak cultures, the rate of job creation was seven times higher, stock price grew twelve times more quickly, and the profit-to-performance ratio was 750 percent higher. Kotter, J., and Heskitt, J. *Corporate Culture and Performance*. New York: Free Press, 1992. Collins, J., and Porras, J. *Built to Last*. New York: HarperCollins, 1994.

16. Collins. *Good to Great*, p. 176.

Chapter Four

1. Hanson, R. E. "A Personal Commitment to Safety." Speech to the Pulp and Paper Safety Association, Tucson, Ariz., June 14, 2004, http://www.weyerhaeuser.com/Company/Media/Speech?dcrID=061420041, copyright © 2004 Weyerhaeuser Company. All rights reserved.

2. "Leading by Example: Roger Corbett's Formula." *Management Today*, Aug. 2004, http://www.aim.com.au/DisplayStory.asp?ID=509.

3. Carey, B. "The Psychology of Cheating." *New York Times*, Apr. 16, 2011.

4. Off-label use is the practice of prescribing pharmaceuticals for a use other than that approved by the Food and Drug Administration. The FDA

approves new drugs for prescription use but does not have the legal authority to regulate the practice of medicine, so physicians may prescribe the drug off label. It is not legal, however, for the pharmaceutical company to promote off-label uses to prescribers.

Chapter Five

1. Gawande, A. *The Checklist Manifesto*. New York: Metropolitan Books, 2009, p. 76.

2. Rosegrant, S., for Leonard, H. B. "Wal-Mart's Response to Hurricane Katrina: Striving for a Public-Private Partnership." Kennedy School of Government Case Program, C16–07–1876.0. Harvard University, 2007.

3. Ibid., p. 9.

4. Ibid.

5. Berkshire Hathaway. *2010 Annual Report*, http://www.berkshirehathaway.com/2010ar/2010ar.pdf.

6. Corporate Executive Board, CFO Executive Board. "Preempting the Risk of Compliance Failures: Five Leading Indicators of Misconduct." 2007.

7. Lichtenstein, N. "Wal-Mart's Authoritarian Culture." *New York Times*, June 21, 2011. Some critics call this a cultlike manipulation of people to abandon their former identities and solidify their allegiance to their new masters. Others maintain that the sense of family connectedness, of which Walmart has always been so proud, is not a corporate manipulation but rather is based on the values of the company's founder, Sam Walton. Despite its enormous size, Walmart has tried to maintain clarity as to the kind of personal values its managers and employees need in order to succeed there. But these values are a mixed bag. One researcher noted that "a patriarchal ethos was written into the Wal-Mart DNA." Certainly the religious authoritarian culture of northwest Arkansas in the 1950s has survived and flourished in a company that is now one of the world's largest employers and is the largest commercial employer in the United States. Lawsuits alleging systematic discrimination against women may in fact stem from this set of corporate values. Those who don't share them may not feel the sense

of connection needed to sustain a committed relationship with the organization.

8. Head, A. "Inside the Leviathan." *New York Review of Books*, Dec. 16, 2004.

Chapter Six

1. Swartz, J. "How I Did It: Timberland's CEO on Standing Up to 65,000 Angry Activists." *Harvard Business Review*, Sept. 2010, 39–43.

2. "Transparency." BusinessDictionary.com, http://www.business dictionary.com/definition/transparency.html.

3. The Corporate Social Responsibility Branding Survey finds that 77 percent of consumers feel that it's important that companies are socially responsible. In a 2010 survey conducted by Landor Associates, Penn Schoen Berland/Burson-Marsteller, evidence shows consumers placing increasing importance on transparency and corporate responsibility. Burson-Marsteller, "Consumers Continue to Prioritize Social Responsibility Across Business Sectors, Despite Recession," Mar. 29, 2010, http://www.burson-marsteller.com/Newsroom/Lists/PressReleases/Disp Form.aspx?ID=748.

4. Research indicates that the fear of retaliation for speaking up is the factor most predictive of the likelihood of misconduct. For example, the CFO Executive Board of the Corporate Executive Board reported: "This fear contributes to the hidden costs of fraud and misconduct—senior executives do not report misconduct more than half the time, and line employees do not report 85% of the misconduct that they observe. These statistics send a critical message to CFOs and other senior leaders: companies must first and foremost ensure that employees have a clear sense of how issues will be handled and create an environment where employees are not afraid to report misconduct." Corporate Executive Board, CFO Executive Board. "Preempting the Risk of Compliance Failures: Five Leading Indicators of Misconduct," 2007.

5. On June 13, 2011, VF Corporation, a leader in branded lifestyle apparel, and Timberland announced that they had signed a definitive merger agreement whereby VF would pay Timberland shareholders forty-three dollars per share, representing a total enterprise value of approximately

$2 billion net of cash acquired. The merger agreement was unanimously approved by both companies' boards of directors.

6. Interview with Robin Giampa, Mar. 9, 2011, Timberland Corporate Offices, Stratham, N.H.

7. Interview with Betsy Blaisdell, Mar. 9, 2011, Timberland Corporate Offices, Stratham, N.H.

8. Swartz, J. "Update from the Amazon." TheBootmakersBlog, Oct. 22, 2009, http://blog.timberland.com/corporate-social-responsibility/update -from-the-amazon/.

9. Interview with Jerry Erwin, Mar. 9, 2011, Timberland Corporate Offices, Stratham, N.H.

10. Timberland. "Responsibility Beyond Factory Walls: Engaging Factory Workers and Strengthening Community," 2009, http://community .timberland.com/Resource_/PageResource/Corporate-Responsibility/ Reporting-Downloads/Beyond-Factory-Walls-2009_Timberland -Report.pdf.

11. Interview with Colleen von Haden, Mar. 9, 2011, Timberland Corporate Offices, Stratham, N.H.

Chapter Seven

1. Collins, J. *Good to Great*. New York: HarperCollins, 2001, p. 176.

2. Broader surveys, such as The Great Place to Work surveys (www .greatplacetowork.com), provide a broad overview of the intangible factors that generate motivation.

SUGGESTED READINGS

Ariely, D. *Predictably Irrational*. New York: HarperCollins, 2009.

Badarraco, J. *Defining Moments*. Boston: Harvard Business School Press, 1997.

Barrett, R. *Liberating the Corporate Soul*. Burlington, Mass.: Butterworth-Heinemann, 1998.

Barrett, R. *Building a Values-Driven Organization*. Burlington, Mass.: Butterworth-Heinemann, 2006.

Bazerman, M., and Tenbrunsel, A. *Blind Spots*. Princeton, N.J.: Princeton University Press, 2011.

Burchell, M., and Robin, J. *The Great Workplace*. San Francisco: Jossey-Bass, 2011.

Coleman, D. *Working with Emotional Intelligence*. New York: Bantam, 1998.

Collins, J. *Good to Great*. New York: HarperCollins, 2001.

Collins, J., and Porras, J. *Built to Last*. New York: HarperCollins, 1994.

Conley, C. *Peak*. San Francisco: Jossey-Bass, 2007.

Gawande, A. *The Checklist Manifesto*. New York: Metropolitan, 2009.

Hsieh, T. *Delivering Happiness*. New York: Business Plus, 2010.

Johnson, L., and Phillips, B. *Absolute Honesty*. New York: AMACOM, 2003.

Kaplan, R., and Norton, D. *Alignment*. Boston: Harvard Business School Press, 2006.

Kofman, F. *Conscious Business*. Boulder, Colo.: Sounds True, 2006.

Kotter, J., and Heskitt, J. *Corporate Culture and Performance*. New York: Free Press, 1992.

Paine, L. *Value Shift*. New York: McGraw-Hill, 2003.

Pink, D. *Drive*. New York: Riverhead, 2009.

Schein, E. *Organizational Culture and Leadership*. San Francisco: Jossey-Bass, 2004.

Stewart, T. *Intellectual Capital*. New York: Currency, 1997.

ACKNOWLEDGMENTS

It has been gratifying to have had so many people lend their support and assistance in the development of this book. Only blessings and insights from above could have led me to such amazing people and have sustained me on this journey.

My longtime friends Richard Barrett and Joan Shafer encouraged me more than a few years ago to write a book and put onto paper the processes and approaches I had developed to help my clients. Their confidence helped me tremendously in making the commitment to start this project. My dear friends Phil Clothier, Chris Gomez, and Ashley Munday from the Barrett Values Centre have provided tremendous support and guidance in the development of the concept of power values. Their openness and sense of transparency is a model for the highest levels of collaboration.

At the point where I was beginning to spin my wheels in crafting a focused book proposal, my friend Bob Phillips introduced me to his agent, Michael Snell, who has been my compass in the writing and development process. Mike provided encouragement, guidance, and wisdom in developing the book's approach and emphasis. Through Mike, I met Betty Rauch, who has been a strong cheerleader and mentor in helping me craft my message. My longtime friend John Case lent his editing expertise in developing the proposal.

My colleague, friend, and co-instructor at Suffolk University, Nir Eisikovits, has been invaluable in his support, lending ideas and clarity to the project. Through Nir's good graces, four research assistants from Suffolk University's Ethics and Public Policy Program have helped me: Jarrod Abbott-Washburn, Avery Struthers, Hannah Berman, and Evan Feinauer.

Deep and sincere thanks go to Genoveva Llosa at Jossey-Bass, who has been such a true believer in this project from the very beginning. Her support and expert guidance in the development process have made this book as strong as it could be. She and the team at Jossey-Bass, including John Maas, Alan Shrader, Bev Miller, and Mary Garrett, have been a pleasure to work with and have added so much to creating the final product you have before you.

Thanks go to Jeff Swartz for granting me access to his wonderful team at the Timberland Company and to Robin Giampa, who coordinated my visits and interviews there.

Thank you to my colleagues at Sage Partners, especially Tom Doorley, John Conway, and Larry Bennigson, for their counsel in the development of the book.

Dear friends and colleagues who provided their wisdom and expertise include Tamar Frankel and David Blaszkowsky, Tony Dolan, Bill Edelman, Stewart Hirsch, and David and Susan Berg provided insight and guidance for key parts of this project.

As I began writing, I was fortunate to have been introduced by my friend Steve Spear to John Elder, who has been a true partner in editing this book. John challenged my assumptions and made sure that every sentence reflects the goals and purpose of this work.

My entire family, and especially my four amazing children—Avishai, Meirav, Ze'ev, and Akiva—made sure I stayed on track with their encouragement and their love. Writing a book adds new meaning to the phrase "labor of love," and they truly kept me going. My biggest thanks and my deepest appreciation go to my wife, Claire, who has been my true partner in this project and in life. Her encouragement, her wisdom, her insight, and her love have made me—and this book—all the better.

ABOUT THE AUTHOR

For nearly twenty years, David Gebler has advised global organizations on how to use their values and culture to drive behavior. He helps organizations reduce people-based risks while improving productivity and corporate reputation. In addition, he has served as an ethics advisor for numerous organizations, advising on policy and corporate standards deployment and drafting codes of conduct and investigation strategies.

He is on the International Advisory Board of Suffolk University's Graduate Program in Ethics and Public Policy, where he coteaches a course in business ethics. A frequent speaker and panelist, Gebler has appeared on CNN, CNBC, and WGBH, discussing topical ethics issues. His first book, *Creating a Culture of Compliance,* was released in 2011. A business lawyer by training, Gebler received his J.D. from the University of California at Davis. As an attorney in private practice with firms such as Proskauer and as corporate counsel for Gamma International, he gained extensive experience on both bank regulatory and software licensing issues. He worked in Israel for CBS Records International as director of business affairs and as a staff lawyer for El Al Israel Airlines.

He can be reached at david@davidgebler.com.

INDEX

A

Acceptance, need for, 46, 63–64

Accountability, 21, 112, 134; and consequences, *91*, 92, 102, 111, 172; cultural influence on, example of, 200n9; desire for, 52; as a dominant value, 81; and engagement, 74, 75; ensuring, 193; from the organization's point of view, 108–110; relevancy of, identifying, example of, 191–192; and responsibility, 102, 116, 121; seeking, at the survival awareness level, 113; in teams, 110; and transparency, 148, 155

Achievement, 12, 36, 64, 72, 73, 81, 83

Acting. *See* Implementation

Action plans, creating and using, steps to, 173. *See also* Culture assessment; Implementation; Strategic planning

Adaptability, 81, 86, 143, 185, 186, 197

Albaugh, James F., 66

Alignment. *See* Cultural alignment

American culture, core part of, 102

Anxiety and fear. *See* Fears and anxieties

Apathy. *See* Disengagement

Apple, 45

Arendt, Steve, 40–41

Ariely, Dan, 39

Asch, Solomon, 45, 71

Aspirations and fears, awareness of, 64, 67. *See also* Awareness levels

Assagioli, Roberto, 202n4

Assessing. *See* Culture assessment

Australia/New Zealand study, 8

Authority, 42, 46, 56, 69, 108, 109, 140

Autonomy: and commitment, 87, *117*, 119, 125, 135–141, 144, 172, 180, 189; need for, 51, 52, 53–54, 55, 56, 84, 87. *See also* Control, desire for

Aversion to loss, 41–42, 69

Awareness levels: concept of, 63–66; from level 1 to 3, described, 68–73; from level 4 to 7, described, 73–79; lower, building up from, 192–195; multiple, operating at, 65; order of, and values at each level, 67. *See also* Communal awareness; Contribution awareness; Engagement awareness; Performance awareness; Relationship awareness; Service awareness; Survival awareness

Awareness levels model. *See* Seven Levels of Awareness (Barrett's model)

B

Backdating stock options, 44–45
Bain, Douglas G., 60, 63
Band-Aid products, 3–4
Barrett, Richard, 64, 67, 77, 202n4
Barrett Values Centre, 8, 203n14
Bartlitt, Fred, 32, 33
BBC broadcast, 56
Behavior: affect of culture on, understanding, need for, 6, 8; benchmarks for, 39; changing, requisite for, 11; and culture, 11–14; deceptive, 4; dysfunctional, as a social norm, 8; stating clear expectations of, 7; subconscious, 36, 37, 63; values and, 5, 11, 18, 22, 23, 64. *See also* Standards of behavior

Behavior roadblocks: avoiding, leaders mindful of, importance of, 56–57; awareness of, need for, 10–11, 33; counterweights to, 35; innate and external factors in, 36–38; as mental switches, 38, 39–56; placing blame vs. removing, 5–7. *See also* Disengagement; Rationalization; Self-deception

Beliefs and principles. *See* Principles
Benchmarks, 39, 176
Berkshire, 121–122
Best Employer study (2008), 8
Best practices, 72, 73, 83, 105, 134, 179, 195
Beth Israel Deaconess Medical Center, 24–25
Blaisdell, Betsy, 153
Blame, 30, 35, 68, 70, 71, 83, 86, 92, 113, 144, 192, 193, 194; placing, vs. removing roadblocks, 5–7
Blindness of leaders, 10
Blindsiding, 9
Boeing, 60–63, 65–66, 70, 71, 73, 75, 76, 77, 80, 85, 109, 164, 170, 172
Boeing Integrated Defense Systems, 66
Bottom line. *See* Profit margin/ bottom line
BP, 13, 32–35, 36, 40–41, 41–42, 182, 197
Browne, John, 34
Buffett, Warren, 121–122
Built to Last (Collins and Porras), 86

Bureaucracy, 17–18, 30, 54, 68, 72, 73, 75, 83, 85, 109, 185, 193
Burke, James, 20, 22, 29, 30
Buy-in, securing, 195

C
Cain, Herman, 42
Caring, 70, 71, 79, 81, 195
"Carson Manufacturing" company, 114–116
Cheating, inclination toward, 39, 103, 104
Clarity, 88, *145*, 151–155, 172, 181, 186, 188, 190, 204n7
Climate surveys, 164, 175
Clinton, Bill, 42
Coaching/mentoring, 77, 186, 191
Code-of-conduct assessment process, example of a, 161–163
Cognitive biases, fundamental, 38. *See also* Disengagement; Rationalization; Self-deception
Collaboration, 73, 77, 78, 133, 149, 151, 186, 194–195
Collins, Jim, 18, 19, 20, 21–22, 77, 86, 172
Command-and-control culture, 66
Commitment: aligning principles and goals, 88, *117*, 120, 124–128, 171–172; assessing, 180–181; at Boeing, 60; cornerstones of, 119; as a counterweight to behavior roadblocks, 35; creating, 87–88, 128–141, 195, 204–205n7; as critical, 5; and cultural alignment, 80, 171, 172, 173; desire for, 6; desired culture and, example of, 191; as a dominant value, 81; examining, with assessment, examples of, 184, 186, 189–190; fairness and, 104; foundations of, 123–124, 135; gauging levels of, 174; as an interdependent value, 29, 30; links principles and goals, 26–27, 171; locking in, 141–144; as a power value, 23–24, 76; profits following from, 142; as the starting point, example of, 30–31; and transparency, 149; understanding interactions among, and integrity and transparency, 171; and why it matters, 7, 120–123
Commitments, taking a serious approach to, 101–102, 108, 172. *See also* Integrity
Communal awareness, 192; assessment examining, example of, 183–184; and balancing self-interest against desire, 93; and commitment, 124, 135, 143; described, 75–77; and the dominance of personal values, 76, 81–83; ensuring values at the level of, 88; example of values of, *67*; key value of, 102; opportunity provided by, 86; and organizations overemphasizing other values, 83–85; power values and, 23, 76

Communication, effective. *See* Open communication

Compassion, 78

Compensation, 52, 53, 55, 73, 82, 177, 178

Competitive advantage, achieving, culture for, 20, 86

Compliance programs: dishonesty in, 6, 8, 9; impact of culture vs. impact of, 9

Condit, Phil, 60, 61

Confirmation bias, 42

Conformity studies, 45–46, 71

Confusion, 30, 68, 72, 83, 87, 105, 106, 109, 134, 143, 184, 187, 193

Connected world, 147

Connection, sense of, 23, 64, 75, *117*, 121, 124, 125, 126, 128–135, 144, 149, 180, 204–205n7

Consequences: accountability and, *91*, 92, 102, 172; building, implementing a plan for, example of, 196; and communal awareness, 76; lack of, 93, 190; from the organization's point of view, 108, 111

Consistency: building, implementing a plan for, example of, 196; and clarity, 152, 172, 188, 190; and communal awareness, 76, 82; creating, 87, 193; culture gap involving, example of, 191; demonstration of, 96; and the elements of culture, 15, 17; from the employee's point of view, 102, 105–108; and fairness, *91*, 92, 97,

101, 102, 112, 116; lack of, 30, 93, 95; and performance awareness, 72; at the relationship level, 113, 114; at the survival level, 112, 113

Contribution awareness, *67*, 77–78

Control, desire for, 55, 68, 69, 72, 74, 120, 128, 136, 137, 142, 147, 149, 166, 189, 193. *See also* Autonomy

Cooperation, 17, 77, 133

Corbett, Roger, 96

Core values: defined, 18; obstacles to living the, 19–20; vs. power values, 24

Corporate Executive Board, 122, 150, 205n4

Corporate responsibility, as a goal, 16–17, 153

Corporate Social Responsibility Branding Survey, 205n3

Cost cutting, 4, 22

Criminal activity, crossing the line to, 49, 61

Cultural alignment, 8, 9, 15, 66, 152; benefits of, 172; building blocks of, 79–85; catalyst for, 22–24; challenges that thwart, 83–85, 95; importance of, 20–22; lack of, frustrations occurring from, 172–173; means of achieving, looking for the, 171–174; model and approach for, need for a, 170–171; path toward, 86–88; sense of, described, 22; three-step process to, 173–196;

two kinds of, 80. *See also* Power values

Cultural transformation: example of, 60–63, 65–66; leadership resulting in, 59–60

Culture: for achieving competitive advantage, 20, 86; adaptability of, 81, 86, 197; American, core part of, 102; behavior and, 11–14; and behavior roadblocks, 38; command-and-control, 66; defined, 7, 200n5; desired, identifying the, 182, 185, 191; elements of, 14–20, 29–30, 38; healthy, foundation of a, 95; impact of, 3–5, 8, 9; importance of, 7–11; and integrity, 96–100; problems with the, 6; role of, in motivation, 52; strong vs. weak, performance of a, 81, 203n15; as a tool, 24; zero-sum, 70. *See also* Goals; Principles; Standards of behavior

Culture assessment: cultural snapshot revealed by a, examples of, 183–185, 188–191; elements of, and methods in, 174–181; overview of, 174; purpose of, 173. *See also* Values assessments

Culture gaps. *See* Gaps

Cultures, risky mix of, 106–107

D

Data collection and analysis. *See* Culture assessment; Values assessments

Decision making, aspects clouding, 36, 37, 38–39. *See also* Disengagement; Rationalization; Self-deception

Deepwater Horizon oil spill disaster, 32–35, 40, 41, 41–42

Delegating, 128, 140, 184, 189, 190, 193, 194

Devil's advocate, use of a, 167

Dilbert cartoon, 123

Disengagement, 13–14, 57, 58, 84; and awareness challenges, addressing, 68; and communal awareness, 77; described, 51–56; preventing, 94, 96; susceptibility to, 63, 79, 93, 94, 103; and transparency, 147, 156

Drilling down, 176

Druyun, Darleen, 61, 70

E

Ebbers, Bernard, 47, 49

Edwards, John, 42

Elkind, Peter, 34

Empire building, 70, 71, 72, 113–114

Engagement: and commitment, 7, *117*, 120, 125, 136, 189; and cultural alignment, 80, 171; dominant values supporting, 81–82; key to, in the alignment process, 195, 196; and micromanagement, 21; and transparency, 156, 162

Engagement awareness, *67*, 74–75, 85, 122, 143, 193

Engagement surveys, 175, 180

Enron, 47

Environmental responsibility, 78,
134, 148, 153, 154

Erwin, Jerry, 157, 159

Ethics Resource Center (ERC), 9

Ethics survey, 164–165

External and innate influences,
36–38

Extrinsic motivation, 52–53, 55, 178

F

Failure, fear of, 63, 188

Fair Factories Clearinghouse, 161

Fairness: and consistency, *91*, 92, 97,
101, 102, 112, 116; from the
employee's point of view,
102–105; ensuring, 193;
importance of, 82; rationalization
involving, 44

Family: as a value, 44, 81; work as,
123, 130, 132

Favoritism, 101, 102, 105, 184

Fears and anxieties, 46, 63–65, 67,
68, 69, 71, 85, 102, 108, 112, 113,
142, 163, 166, 174, 188, 192,
202n4, 205n4

Federal Bureau of Investigation
(FBI), 20, 29

Feedback: lack of, effect of, 51, 52;
need for, 84

Feedback loop, positive, creating a,
30

Financial scandals, culture and
rationalizations involved in,
example of, 47–49

Firefighting, 72, 83, 185, 193

Flywheel effect, 21–22

Focus groups, 81, 164, 165, 178, 180

Fortune magazine, investigations by,
27, 34

Fortune's "100 Best Companies to
Work For" list, 8, 86

G

Gap, The, 26, 171

Gaps, 18–19, 21, 28, 85, 86, 101,
151, 179, 180, 182, 185–186, 191

Generalizations, 43

Giampa, Robin, 153

Goals, 63; alignment of, 17, 22, 23,
66, 87; assessing, 176–178; as
attributes characterizing
organizations, 59; commitment
links principles and, 26–27, 171;
as an element of culture, 15,
16–17, 20, 38; gaps between,
identifying, 182; integrity links
standards and, 25, 172; and
looking for alignment, 171; and
power values, *23*; and principles,
aligning, 25, 80, 88, *117*, 119,
120, 124–141, 171–172; questions
to ask about, 97; rationalization
and, 50; revealing, with
assessment, examples of, 183,
188; and standards, aligning, 25,
87, *91*, 97, 101–116, 172; taking
stock of, 98–99

Goggins, Colleen, 21, 29, 36–37

Good to Great (Collins), 21–22

Green Working Group, 159

Greenpeace, 145, 146, 153, 156, 157
Group norms. *See* Social norms
Gulf of Mexico disaster. *See* BP

H
Haden, Colleen von, 162
Hanson, Richard, 92
Hayes, Ronny, 118
Hayward, Tony, 32, 33, 34, 35,
    36–37
Health and safety issues. *See* Safety
    issues
Heskitt, James, 86
Hewitt Associates, 8
Hierarchical organizations, 149
Hierarchy of human needs, 23, 64,
    67, 202n4
Honesty, 11, 25, 27, 28, 81, 149,
    175. *See also* Integrity;
    Transparency
Human needs: hierarchy of, 23, 64,
    67, 202n4; of others, balancing
    self-interest and the, 57, 66;
    unfulfilled, linked to anxieties or
    fears, 46, 63–64, 68, 85
Humility, 78
Hurricane Dennis, 40
Hurricane Katrina, 117, 118–119,
    135

I
Identity, collective, sense of, 130,
    204n7. *See also* Connection, sense
    of
Implementation: approaches to,
    192–196; purpose of, 174

Inclusion, need for, 46, 63–64, 71,
    125
Inconsistency, issue of. *See*
    Consistency
Individual values. *See* Personal
    values
Individuation, 202n4
Information 24/7, access to, 147,
    148
Information flow, maintaining,
    149–150
Innate and external influences,
    36–38
Innovation, 17, 25, 70, 75, 83, 120,
    185
Integrity, 62; aligning goals and
    standards, *91*, 97, 101–116, 172;
    assessing, 180; building, key to,
    97–98; causal connection between
    transparency and, 181–182; as a
    counterweight to behavior
    roadblocks, 35; crises of,
    organizational successes creating,
    106–107; as critical, 5, 186; and
    cultural alignment, 172, 173; and
    culture, 96–100; defining, 25, 95;
    developing, as a first step toward
    alignment, 87, 106; as a dominant
    value, 81, 82; ensuring, in
    addition to creating commitment,
    124; examining, with assessment,
    examples of, 184, 190; first step to
    establishing, 102; instilling, steps
    to, 112–116; as an interdependent
    value, 29, 30, 31; links goals and
    standards, 25, 172; maintaining,

Integrity (*Cont'd*)
issue of, 3; opportunity to practice, example of, 50; as a power value, 23–24, 76, 104; profits following from, 142; of quality engineers, pressure facing, 3; and relationship awareness, 113–116; as the starting point, example of, 30; understanding interactions among, and transparency and commitment, 171; and why it matters, 94–96
Interviews, 55, 81, 108, 109, 127, 131, 132, 178, 180
Intrinsic motivation, 53, 55, 82, 87, 178, 180–181
Isolation, 84, 160, 166–167

J
Jobs, Steve, 45
Johnson & Johnson (J&J), 3–4, 5–6, 7, 8, 16, 18, 19, 20–22, 27, 28–29, 30, 36, 76, 85, 170, 182, 197, 199n2
Johnson, Robert Wood, 199n2
Johnson's Baby Shampoo, 4
Jung, Carl, 202n4

K
Kahneman, Daniel, 41
Kaplan, Robert, 19, 20
Keltner, Dacher, 42–43
Kennedy School of Government, 118
Kerviel, Jérôme, 46
Kimes, Mina, 27
Knowledge workers, 52, 55, 120
Kotter, John, 86

L
Leather Working Group, 154
Levels of awareness. *See* Awareness levels
Levy, Paul, 24–25
Lewin, Kurt, 12, 38, 63
Lewis, Jessica, 118
Liked by others, need for being, 46, 48, 63–64
Listening, importance of, 142
Lockheed Martin, 60
Long-term perspective, 78
Loss avoidance, 41–42
"Lothrop Financial" company, 6, 7, 8, 9, 85
Loyalty, sense of, 129, 130, 135. *See also* Commitment

M
Macando project, 33, 41
Making a difference, 77, 78, 79, 126, 188, 192
Maslow, Abraham, 22–23, 63, 67, 202n4
Massachusetts Institute of Technology (MIT), 34
Matrixed organizations, 149
McDonnell Douglas, 62, 65
MCI Communications, 48
McNeil Consumer Healthcare, 4, 5–6, 19, 20–21, 29
McNeil, Janie, 118–119
McNerney, Jim, 63, 65–66, 67, 70, 71, 73, 75, 76, 77, 80, 109, 164, 172
Mental switches, 13, 38, 39. *See also* Behavior roadblocks

Mentoring/coaching, 77, 186, 191

Mergers, 4

Micromanagement, 69, 138

Milgram, Stanley, 56, 69

Misconduct, reporting, 9, 122, 165

Mission and goals. *See* Goals

MIT (Massachusetts Institute of Technology), 34

Motivations: core, and contribution awareness, 77–78; deeper, probing, 175; dominant values serving as, 81–82; extrinsic, 52–53, 55, 178; intrinsic, 53, 55, 82, 87, 178, 180–181; mapping, 174; understanding, importance of, 196; unfulfilled needs and fears as, 63–64. *See also* Intrinsic motivation

Motrin, 4

Myers, David, 46, 47–49, 56, 69

N

Needs. *See* Human needs

Negative values: awareness level containing the largest percentage of, 72; having too many, challenge of, 85; and positive values, existence of both, 68, 176, 197

Neurological influences, 38

Nordstrom, 7

"Northern Defense" company, 51–52, 72, 84, 85, 168–169, 173, 183–187, 193–195

Norton, David, 19, 20

O

Objectives. *See* Goals

Occupational Safety and Health Administration (OSHA), 114, 116, 193

Off-label use, 107, 203–204n4

"100 Best Companies to Work For" list, 8, 86

Open communication, 6, 28, 70, 88, 113, 148, 186, 192, 193–194. *See also* Transparency

"Operations Academy," 34

Optimism, excessive, 41

Organizational goals: assessing, 176–177, 178; meeting personal goals and, issue of, 16, 97. *See also* Goals

Organizational values: assessing, 175–176; within each level of awareness, *67*; identifying, 80–81. *See also* Values

Overconfidence, 41

P

Pandora's box, 100

Paradoxes, 42–43, 103, 120

Peer pressure, 44, 179. *See also* Social norms

Performance awareness, *67*, 72–73, 83, 102, 105, 109, 135, 140–141, 142, 193

Performance evaluations, 178

Performance, revving up, tool for, 24

Personal goals: assessing, 177–178; meeting assigned goals and, issue of, 16, 97; rationalizing, 50. *See also* Goals

Personal values: actions based on, 11; assessing, 175; dominance of, at the communal awareness level, 76, 81–83; within each level of awareness, *67*; identifying, 80–81. *See also* Values

Pfizer, 4, 21, 22

"PharmX" company, 106–107, 109, 110

Planning. *See* Strategic planning

Point of view: employee's, fairness and consistency from the, 102–108; organization's, accountability and consequences from the, 108–111

Politeness, 43, 113

Porras, Jerry, 86

Power: need for, 46; paradox of, 42–43

Power values: assessments examining the, examples of, 184–185, 189–191; and communal awareness, 23, 76; core values vs., 24; described, 22–29; as interdependent, 29; relevant, identifying, 182, 186–187, 191–192; separately addressing the, basis for, 29–31. *See also* Commitment; Integrity; Transparency

Predictability, need for, 96

Principles, 4, 63; alignment of, 20–21, 22, 23, 66, 87; assessment of, 174–176; as attributes characterizing organizations, 59; commitment links goals and, 26–27, 171; defining, clarity in, importance of, 152, 153, 154; as an element of culture, 15, 17–18, 20, 38; enforcement of, 160–163; gaps between, identifying, 182; and goals, aligning, 25, 80, 88, *117*, 119, 120, 124–141, 171–172; and looking for alignment, 171; and power values, *23*, 24; revealing, with assessment, examples of, 183–184, 188–189; and standards, aligning, 25, 88, 150–169; transparency links standards and, 27–29, 172. *See also* Values

Profit margin/bottom line: clarity in balancing, with principles, 154, 155; committing to other goals besides the, 142; excessive focus on the, 69–70, 112; quality/safety vs., 3, 27, 32, 33–34, 36, 40–41, 114–116, 158

Project RED, 26

Proprietary document scandal, 60

Psychology, role of, 22–23, 38

Psychosynthesis, 202n4

Q

Quality issues, 3, 4, 5, 6, 16, 18, 19, 20–21, 22, 27, 121, 158, 179, 184, 186

Quality professionals, pressure facing, 3, 19

R

Rationality and rationalization, line between, 46–47

Rationalization, 13, 37–38, 57, 60, 68, 72–73, 77; described, 43–50; paths of, 44; preventing, 94, 96; rationality and, line between, 46–47; susceptibility to, 63, 79, 93, 94, 103, 104, 105; and transparency, 147

Realities, creating our own, 39, 43. *See also* Disengagement; Rationalization; Self-deception

Recalls, 4, 20, 27, 28–29

Recognition, 36, 46, 71

Relationship awareness, *67*, 70–72, 102, 113–116, 138–140, 142, 169, 192–193, 193–194

Relationships, need for, 202n4

Reporting misconduct, 9, 122, 165

Reputation, false sense of security provided by, 157

Respect, 28, 46, 71, 72, 81, 109, 113, 125, 130, 131, 138, 139, 140, 142, 163, 182

Responsibility, 11, 29; and accountability, 102, 116, 121; assuming more, expectation of, 105, 124; and bureaucracy, 193; and commitment, 87, *117*, 120, 125, 126, 136, 144, 189; corporate, 16–17, 153; desire for, 52; as a dominant value, 81; and engagement, 75; environmental, 78, 134, 148, 153, 154; and levels of awareness, 71, 72, 73, 74, 75,

78; paradox involving, 42; power values influencing, 24; social, 78, 134, 148, 205n3; taking, vs. disengaging, 54–55, 56, 74, 87; transferring, to others, problem with, 56; and transparency, 149

Retail chains, 26

Retaliation, 7, 9, 66, 72, 150, 164, 205n4

Retention levels, evaluating, 180

Riker, Donald, 29

Risk aversion, 41–42, 68, 69

Risk, tool for managing, 24

Roadblocks. *See* Behavior roadblocks

Root causes, getting to the, 62, 67, 112, 160, 161, 164, 167–169, 173

S

S&P 500, 8

Safe space, creating a, for raising issues, 7, 30, 160, 163–166, 167. *See also* Transparency

Safety issues, 4, 7, 19, 20, 27, 28–29, 30, 32, 33–34, 35, 36, 40–41, 91–92, 114–116, 158

Sarbanes-Oxley legislation, 147–148, 167

Schein, Edgar, 200n5

Scott, Lee, 117–118

Sears, Michael, 60–61, 70

Securities and Exchange Commission, 45

Self-actualization, capacity for, 64, 65, 202n4

Self-awareness, 64, 65, 79, 169, 196–197

Self-deception, 13, 57, 60–61, 68, 77, 147; described, 39–43; preventing, 94, 96; susceptibility to, 63, 79, 93, 94, 103, 104; types of, 41–42

Self-esteem, 46, 53, 68, 72, 79, 112, 202n4

Self-fulfillment, achieving, 64

Self-interest and needs of others, balancing, 57, 66

Service awareness, *67*, 78–79

Seven Levels of Awareness (Barrett's model), 64, 67–79, 202n5. *See also* Awareness levels

Sexual discrimination, 61, 204n7

Sexual harassment, 61

Shefrin, Hersh, 41

Shell, 34

Silence, culture of, 66

Silicon Valley, 45

Silo mentality, 71, 73, 133

Six Sigma program, 186

Slippery slopes, 25, 50, 103, 105, 111

Social networks, 148, 149

Social norms, 7, 8, 12, 18–19, 39, 45–46, 49, 71, 93, 94, 116, 178, 179

Social responsibility, 78, 134, 148, 205n3

Sociopaths, 12

Southwest Airlines, 7

Speaking up, factors inhibiting, 6–7, 28, 66, 71

Spitzer, Eliot, 42

St. Joseph aspirin, 3

Standards of behavior, 63; alignment of, 22, 23, 66, 87; assessing, 178–180; as attributes characterizing organizations, 59; credibility of, defined, 103; decline in, 3, 4; defining, clarity in, importance of, 152, 154; as an element of culture, 15, 18–19, 20, 38; enforcement of, 160; gaps between actions and, identifying, 179, 180; and goals, aligning, 25, 87, *91*, 97, 101–116, 172; integrity links goals and, 25, 172; and looking for alignment, 171; and power values, *23*; and principles, aligning, 25, 88, *145*, 150–169, 172; questions to ask about, 97; revealing, with assessment, examples of, 183, 188; taking stock of, 99–100; transparency links principles and, 27–29, 172

Starbucks, 7

Stereotypes, 43

Stock options, backdating, 44–45

Stonecipher, Harry, 42, 62, 63

Strategic planning: case examples of, 183–192; overview of, 181–182; purpose of, 173; three-step process for analysis in, 182, 185–187, 191–192; using assessment results in, examples of, 183–185, 188–191

Strong vs. weak cultures, performance of, 81, 203n15

Subconscious behaviors, 36, 37, 63. *See also* Disengagement; Rationalization; Self-deception

Subcultures, 65, 181

Success, need for, 46, 63–64

Successful organizations, 197

Sullivan, Scott, 47, 48, 49

Surprises, dislike of, 95, 106

Surveys, 28, 122, 133, 143, 164, 174, 175, 178, 180

Survival awareness, *67*, 68–70, 83, 102, 112–113, 137–138, 141–142, 192

Survival need, 202n4

Survival-of-the-fittest attitude, 70

Swartz, Jeff, 145, 146, 155, 156, 158

T

Team players, 189

Teamwork, 74, 75, 80, 110, 134, 143, 149, 186, 194–195

Texas City refinery, 34

3M, 63

Thunder Horse oil platform, 40

Tiger teams, 131

Timberland Company, 16–17, 78, 134, 145–146, 151, 152–154, 155, 156–159, 160–163, 170, 205–206n5

Toyota, 157

Toyota production system, 179

Trade-offs, 33

Transformation process, 202n4

Transparency: aligning standards and principles, *145*, 150–169; assessing, 181; building, as a third step toward alignment, 88; building blocks of, 159–169; causal connection between integrity and, 181–182; clarity and, 151–155; as a counterweight to behavior roadblocks, 35; as critical, 5; and cultural alignment, 172, 173; definitions of, 147; examining, with assessment, examples of, 184–185, 186, 190–191; expectation of, 148–149; heart of, 148; and information flow, 149–150; as an interdependent value, 29, 30, 31; journey to, 150–151; links standards and principles, 27–29, 172; opportunity to practice, example of, 49–50; as a power value, 23–24, 76; profits following from, 142; as the starting point, example of, 30; truthfulness and, 151, 155–159; understanding interactions among, and commitment and integrity, 171; and why it matters, 146–151, 205n4

Trial-and-error, 53

Trust: and commitment, 126–127, 128; earning, improving, example of, 195–196; foundations for, 96; heart of what generates, 148; importance of, 70, 76, 82–83, 109, 191; and the power values, 24; quantifiable value of, 70; and transparency, 159, 162, 190, 191

Truthfulness, 27, 41, 88, 109, *145*, 151, 155–159, 160, 163, 166, 172, 181, 192

Tversky, Amos, 41

Tylenol, 4, 19, 20, 28, 29, 30

U

Unfair treatment, issue of. *See*
Fairness
U.S. Air Force, 61
U.S. Congress, 4, 24
U.S. Department of Agriculture
(USDA) standards, 157
U.S. Food and Drug
Administration, 4, 20, 107,
203–204n4
"USZ" corporation, 43, 130–133,
164–166

V

Values: behavior and, 5, 11, 18, 22,
23, 64; and behavior roadblocks,
39, 40, 43; competing, attempts
at balancing, truthfulness in, 157,
158–159; connected, restoring, by
focusing on one starting point,
29–31; critical, 5; defining, 17, 22;
dominating at the communal
level, 76, 81–83; goals and, 16;
identifying, means of, 80–81;
within levels of awareness, 64, 67,
68–79; overlap in, too little,
83–85; selective application of,
decision making involved in,
37–38; shared, benefit of, 24, 76,
86. *See also* Core values; Negative
values; Power values; Principles;
specific values
Values assessments, 80–81, 83, 102,
108, 112, 124, 126, 143, 175–176,
180, 181, 183–185, 188–191, 195,

203n14. *See also* Culture
assessment
Values gap. *See* Gaps
VF Corporation, 205–206n5
Virtuous people, 12
Vision: compelling, desire for a,
129, 184; responsible, 78; shared,
76, 77
Visionary goals, 16–17

W

Walking the talk, 25, 76, 87, 97,
116, 172
Walmart, 117–119, 135, 171–172,
204–205n7
Walton, Sam, 204n7
Watchdog agencies/groups,
evaluations by, 181
"Watching their backs," 113, 126,
189. *See also* Commitment
Weak cultures, performance of
strong cultures vs., 81, 203n15
Weak spots, compensating for,
173
"Western Financial" company,
55–56, 92, 94, 98–99, 111,
125–128, 140–141, 152, 169, 173,
177, 187–192, 195–196
Weyerhaeuser, 91–92
Win-at-any-cost attitude, 70, 188
Woolsworth (Australia), 96
WorldCom, 8, 13, 46, 47–49, 56, 69

Z

Zero-sum culture, 70, 168